A BLUE PRINT FOR BUILDING WEALTH THROUGH THE TAX CODE

SOLUTIONS FOR RETIREMENT, BUSINESS, AND REAL ESTATE TAX PROBLEMS

ANDREW KEEHN

ISBN: 979-8-35096-929-0 (print)
ISBN: 979-8-35096-930-6 (eBook)

DISCLAIMER

The Material discussed is meant for general information purposes only. Although the information is gathered from sources believed to be reliable, please note that individual situations vary. Consult your tax, legal, or accounting professional regarding your individual situation.

This book is not intended to provide fiduciary, tax, or legal advice and cannot be used to avoid tax penalties; nor is it intended to market, promote, or recommend any tax plan or arrangement.

Contents

My Philosophy and Why It Matters

I have spent thousands and thousands of hours learning everything I possibly can about taxes, the stock market, estate planning, asset protection, life insurance, and the like. My daily routine consists of continuous learning.

I have read countless articles and watched videos that are outright lies, twisted facts, or misunderstood concepts about every financial strategy and product I could find.

The reason is simple.

I believe the tax and financial industries are broken, and we have intentionally been dumbed down and not given financial education. And why should we be given financial education? The more we know, the more powerful and financially free we can be. The lack of education forces us to continue shifting our wealth to banks, Wall Street, and the government. It keeps them in control and us enslaved.

Everywhere you look, someone is trying to take your money. Banks want you to put your money into their vaults. Wall Street wants you to give them money from every paycheck into a 401(k). The government wants your money, so they keep implementing new taxes. Credit card companies charge you outrageous fees to use their cards.

I view finances from a mathematical perspective and have no emotional attachment to one product or strategy. Any opinion I have is due to the thousands of hours of research and experience I have in investments, real estate, and tax strategies.

Much of my practice is dedicated to helping my clients keep the money they already make while reducing risks. This allows me to help them build the most holistic financial plan possible. There are an incredible number of ways to make money. Making money isn't the hard part. The hard part is keeping money.

For the record, I was licensed as a registered investment advisor, and I managed money. I believe the stock market can be a good way to create wealth, but it takes dedication to understanding global politics, taxes, interest rates, and the market itself. It takes time and dedication to understand many companies' balance sheets, future, and how the CEO runs the corporation. The idea of simply putting money into an account and "holding it for the long term" does not work. You do not become wealthy by keeping your money trapped in an account and watching the paper value of that account go up and down throughout your lifetime.

Wealth gets destroyed from market losses, compounding fees, compounding taxes, opportunity costs, and leaving your money sit idle. Wealth is created through the velocity of money, cash flow, leverage, and paying as few taxes as possible. This book is written to show you how to preserve your wealth, protect your assets, and create Tax-Free Passive Cash-Flow.

Family Banking System:
Control the Banking System in Your Life and Create Untaxable Generational Wealth.

Borrowing money seems to be one of America's favorite pastimes, and sending our wealth to others through the interest we pay is one of the biggest destroyers of wealth. When we look at the spending habits of Americans, approximately 20 percent of our money is spent on transportation, 30 percent is spent on housing, and 45 percent is spent on living—clothes, groceries, charity, insurance, cars, vacations, etc.

Many of these items are financed by credit cards or bank loans. Ultimately, 30 to 35 percent of our money goes to banks and credit cards in the form of interest. The lending institutions have taught us to focus on the interest rate we pay, not the volume of interest we pay. The interest *volume* we pay is more detrimental than the interest *rate* we pay.

You may be thinking, "My house is only 3 percent or 6" percent," but your focus has been detracted from the real costs, which include the volume of interest you are paying to other institutions **AND** the opportunity cost of all the future wealth you lose by giving all this money to other institutions. Let's check out the numbers on a $300,000 home loan.

Here is the scenario.
Let's assume you have a $300,000 mortgage on a new home and the interest rate is 6%.

By the end of year one you'll pay off $3,684 of principal and pay the bank $17,890 of interest. By year 7, you'll pay off $31,082.81 of principal and you'll pay the bank $120,005. In the first 7 years, 79 percent of your money goes to the bank.

What happens after five or seven years? Most people buy a new house and start the process over. Why do banks want you to refinance your house? Because it starts the whole process over. You may be paying less per month, but the bank is getting more of your money through interest.

"But my house has appreciated, and now it's worth a lot more." If you look at it from a broader perspective, when you buy a house to live in, you give away most, if not all, of the value you gain.

Most of the value you gain is lost to the real estate commission you pay when you sell the house and the repairs you make to the house when you own it. Think about what repairs cost on a house. About $5,000 to $10,000 is what you pay for new heat and air. What about a new roof? Even if insurance pays for it, due to a hailstorm, you are likely to have a $2,000-$5,000 deductible.

A new water heater can cost you $1,000-$2,000. A dishwasher can easily be $500-$1000. What about a new driveway or repairs? A new sump pump? The point is, home ownership is expensive. Because of these expenses, the likelihood of your personal residence ever helping you build wealth is quite low.

The problem isn't necessarily the interest itself. The bigger problem lies in the fact that you finance your lifestyle through banking institutions and shift the value of your money, and all future value of your money, to these institutions. The alternative to paying interest to other institutions is to pay cash. But there are two problems:

1. Saving the amount of money needed simply isn't feasible,
2. When you pay cash, there is still an interest cost. There may not be an interest payment, but there is an interest cost, which I will discuss later in the book.

But I pay cash. I don't pay interest!

Are you one of the lucky ones who pays cash? You may not have an interest *PAYMENT*, but you still have an interest *COST*. When you pay cash, you're still financing the items you buy because you're giving up returns that could have been earned on that money. You're giving up the current value and all the future value this money will provide.

What is a *Family Banking System?*

A *Family Banking System* is a family business formed explicitly to provide financing funds to family members. It helps you build wealth using the same financial principles banks and corporations use, such as constant cash flow, positive arbitrage, velocity of money, compounding interest, and nontaxable wealth.

It provides a source of funding that can be more flexible and customized than conventional bank financing. It provides opportunities for businesses in the form of cash flow and capital financing, ultimately ending their dependence on conventional banks. It protects your family and creates generational wealth without the government, or outside financial institutes, such as credit cards or conventional banks.

It is referred to as a "bank" because it mimics the workings of a conventional bank. The benefits go directly to the family instead of another institution.

This is one of the key financial strategies that have helped families such as the Rothschilds and Rockefellers to maintain their wealth and continue growing their wealth. There are many financial vehicles you can use to achieve this system, but one financial vehicle is superior. If you want to learn more about this system, jump to the back of the book.

Have You Outgrown Your Tax Professional?

Many people do not receive adequate tax-saving advice from their current tax professional, and they pay more taxes than they are legally required to pay. The reason is simple: Most accountants are tax accountants and tax preparers, not tax strategists. They see their job as taking the information you give them and filling in boxes. They are simply reporting history.

Sure, some tax professionals are good at putting the correct numbers in the correct boxes on the proper forms. But oftentimes, they don't adequately verify the information they are given. When these numbers are not verified, the tax returns are not done correctly.

Perhaps your tax professional will try to rack up as many deductions or tax "write-offs" as they can find for you. Tax "write-offs" are components that reduce your taxes, but they are not tax strategies. A tax write-off is nothing more than an expense you incur to run your business, and it lowers your taxable income for the year. It's not a dollar-for-dollar deduction against your taxes. It's a deduction against your income.

Yes, there is phenomenal value in having a great tax preparer as part of your team. They have an important skill. But too often, even at the CPA level, tax preparers generally don't do the kind of proactive, strategic planning that will help you save money on taxes in future years. It's simply because their skill is as tax preparers, not tax strategists.

Many accountants list "tax planning" as one of their services. But what do they mean by "tax planning?" In some cases, they'll sit down with you sometime in November or December to see how much tax you can expect to owe. That's not planning; that's projecting.

If you're looking at a tax bill, they'll suggest buying some equipment or a new vehicle before the end of the year. Or maybe they'll suggest setting up a qualified retirement plan and kicking the tax can down the road.

Does that sound familiar? All these short-term measures come at a cost. These deductions may be effective at reducing your taxable income for one year, but they hurt your overall wealth-building abilities and can lead you down a very counterproductive path. Some deductions force you to spend unnecessary dollars to save dimes and create debt. This debt reduces your cash flow due to monthly payments. This cash flow could be used to grow your business, pay off debt, or create memories with your family.

Other deductions, such as 401(k)s and IRAs, lock up your capital, risk your money, and build tax liabilities for you down the road. Tax-deductible retirement plans end up being an IOU to the IRS. You have no idea how high taxes will go or how much of that trapped money you'll get to keep.

Now, I'm not saying you should never buy new equipment or new vehicles. You run a business. Sometimes, these are necessary expenses. I'm simply saying, do not do this just to save some money on taxes. If these deductions are your tax professional's "go-to" strategies, then it's a good indication they are a tax preparer, not tax a strategists.

Being a tax preparer doesn't make them a bad person. It's just that for these people, reducing your taxes isn't their job. Their expertise is not in reducing your taxes, just as I do not have the expertise and skill for bookkeeping and auditing financial statements.

Do you want someone who is constantly looking backwards, or do you want someone who is going to constantly look forward? Me? I want someone in my copilot's seat, looking forward.

> As you read through this book, I want you to ask yourself, "has my CPA ever suggested I use this strategy? Why not? What else are they are not telling me?"

Why Tax Planning Is Important

Over your lifetime, if you make money, taxes will likely be your single biggest expenditure and one of the biggest thieves of your wealth. For most people, income tax, social security and Medicare tax take 25-30 percent of their money. This means they are working two hours every day for the government. Between work, sports, and school activities, do you even spend two hours a day with your kids? Most parents don't.

How excited would you be if your financial advisor could get you an 8–10 percent return a year, and you never ever lost those gains? What if those gains were tax-free and there was zero risk? I know you'd be excited. I hear people brag all the time about their financial advisor growing their portfolio by 10 or 15 percent. But these are paper gains. These gains can easily be lost by the time they take the money out.

Now, what if, instead of 8–10 percent paper return, you got 20–30 percent real return every single year with little effort and no risk? You'd probably put your money into an investment with those returns in a heartbeat.

Good tax planning can reduce your taxes by 15 percent, 20 percent, 30 percent, and more. These are real gains, not paper gains. These are real gains that compound year after year after year with no risk and very little effort. When our clients come on board, there is always an initial investment. But their return on their investment usually ranges from 200 to 500 percent.

Tax Preparer *vs.* Tax Strategist

There's a world of difference between tax preparation and strategic tax *planning.*

Tax preparation involves gathering documents and reporting on history. It's a once-a-year event. Strategic tax planning is an ongoing process that involves careful consideration of your current and future financial situation.

Strategic tax planning involves developing a *comprehensive strategy for minimizing overall tax liabilities* while complying with tax laws and regulations. It involves coordinating long-term tax reduction strategies to reduce taxes over a lifetime. You're seeing around corners and thinking years, decades, and even generations ahead into the future.

Tax preparation does not take your entire financial picture into consideration and forces you to make short-term financial decisions in isolation, without regard for the long-term tax ramifications. Strategic tax planning looks at your entire financial plan and how the entire tax situation will be affected by a single transaction or by multiple transactions. Tax preparers work in a silo. Strategic tax planners, on the other hand, work together as a team of advisors.

Without a strategic tax plan, individuals and businesses will miss opportunities to reduce their tax liabilities. This leads to more taxes, lower profitability, less competitiveness, and a lot more stress in the long run.

In the end, a tax preparer is looking at the past through a rear-view mirror. You can't change the past, so nothing can be done to help. You should always be looking through the windshield for the next opportunity or obstacle.

> **Tax preparation is an EXPENSE, and records how much money you owe the IRS. Tax planning is an INVESTMENT and helps you give less money to the IRS**

How Much Does Your CPA Cost You Each Year?

Let's look at how much your tax preparer is costing you every year. Now, you may be excited because your tax preparer is cheap, and perhaps you even get a refund every year, no matter how much money you're bringing in. Just because you are getting money back every year, doesn't mean you should be.

Suppose your tax professional doesn't charge you a lot for their services. Let's suppose the going rate is $1,500 for your tax situation, but your tax professional only charges you $500. Remember, you get what you pay for. A good tax professional for business owners should never be cheap.

Overpayment	Interest Rate	5 Years	10 Years	20 Years	30 Years
$10,000	5%	$68,218	$142,933	$361,876	$757,153
$20,000	5%	$142,104	$298,807	$758,004	$1,514,306
$30,000	5%	$213,156	$448,210	$1,137,006	$2,271,459

The first column in the chart refers to the amount of taxes you're overpaying every single year due to improper tax-planning, or no tax-planning. Let's pretend for a moment that you have a good tax planner who saves you a lot of taxes because he or she understands the tax code is written as a roadmap to help you grow your wealth and to not pay taxes.

Instead of paying the IRS, you reinvest your money. You could reinvest that money into income-generating assets like businesses or real estate. In that case, the opportunity cost of you overpaying your taxes every year is infinite.

But let's say you don't like real estate and you're not interested in buying other businesses. You can put those tax-savings into a compounding account that grows at least 5–7 percent every year without risking your money, and you'll never have to pay taxes on the growth of this account.

Unlike other accounts, this account gives you access to your money, and access to the growth of your money, without paying taxes or penalties. Not only does it give you access to your money tax-free, but you can also leverage this account to create your Family Banking System and keep your money growing uninterrupted, even though you're using your money. This simple strategy can put hundreds of thousands or millions of dollars back into your pockets throughout your lifetime. What is a Family Banking System? I've dedicated the end of this book to answering that question.

Are you ready to take tax planning seriously and learn some strategies your current tax advisor isn't showing you? Let's go!

Chapter 1
Execute the Basics to Perfection

Before we get to the advanced stuff, let's review the fundamentals. First, the single biggest factor that causes business owners to overpay taxes is disorganization and bad bookkeeping.

The single biggest factor that causes retirees to overpay taxes in retirement is the contribution of the bulk of their retirement "savings" to a 401(k), IRA, or other qualified account.

As business owners, we are terrible at recordkeeping. It's a boring task, and it tends to be a skill we undervalue and an expense we don't want to pay for. We always seem to have too many other things going on, and we ignore bookkeeping. But it's critical. Bookkeeping is the single best tax strategy you can have, and it's critical for a successful business. About 95% of the customers that come to me would fail an IRS audit simply due to their horrific record keeping and bookkeeping.

Good recordkeeping is the foundation necessary to execute all the other strategies we're going to talk about over the course of this book. It will help you identify more deductible expenses. It is easy to miss tax deductions if you don't have organized documentation. Without good records, you won't be able to qualify for some of the most important tax breaks the law allows.

Bad bookkeeping leads to disorganization, which leads to tax consequences, including missed deadlines, inaccurate or incomplete tax returns, and missed deductions or credits. That doesn't mean I want you to get personally bogged down in the minutiae of bookkeeping every day.

As a business owner, your value is in running your business and creating processes to help your business generate revenue. As the business owner, you should know what good bookkeeping looks like! And you should know all your numbers in detail. You should understand where your money is going and how your expenses are benefiting your business. Make sure your balance sheet and profit and loss statement are reconciled at least quarterly, preferably monthly, so that you can make sound business decisions based on your numbers. This is one of the differences that distinguish a business owner from an employee that works for his business.

Do yourself a favor and hire a *good* bookkeeper. Bookkeeping operations are a *staff* function. Not an executive function. You'll be more organized and less stressed, and you'll make more money. Then review your books every month.

> ## Good bookkeeping is an investment. Bad bookkeeping is a very expensive liability. It can cost you years and opportunity cost.

The High Cost of Being Disorganized

Being organized is critical because it not only helps you save money on taxes but also enables you to create more wealth and protect your rear end if you ever get audited. Organization includes keeping track of all receipts, invoices, and other financial and legal documents related to your business, even when applying for a loan.

Additional Benefits of Organization and Good Bookkeeping

Maintaining separate accounts helps to reinforce the corporate veil. Separate accounts improve your bookkeeping and provide better records to improve your tax savings and returns. Proper bookkeeping also provides you with audit protection, improves decision making for business owners and lenders, and reduces stress.

Audit Defense

If you're unprepared and can't prove your stance on an issue to an auditor, they can disallow your deductions and your tax strategies. This can lead to penalties and interest and increase your chances of audits for previous and proceeding years.

During an audit, the IRS may request to review a variety of business documents, including the following:

- Financial statements, such as balance sheets and income statements
- Previous tax returns
- Sales and purchase invoices
- Bank and credit card statements
- Payroll records
- Employment tax records, including forms W2 and 1099
- Contracts and agreements
- Depreciation schedules

- Corporate books

If you cannot provide these requested documents, or if the documents you provide are incomplete or inaccurate, the IRS may disallow certain deductions, credits, or tax strategies. Those disallowances can be very expensive setbacks.

When you have great records and you get audited, the IRS will likely be quickly in and out of your life. If your activities and expenses are properly documented, the tax collector will have difficulty making a case for any charges.

Conversely, by not having the documentation to support what you report on your tax return, you're indicating to an auditor that you're sloppy, unorganized, and possibly lying.

A solid income statement and balance sheet and solid recordkeeping for all mileage, travel, and entertainment expenses communicate to the auditor that you're serious about keeping good records and that you treat your business like a real business, not a hobby.

Tip:
Document of all your mileage. Keep track of every meeting, who you're with, and why you're there. This includes dinners and traveling. Deduct or depreciate all the ordinary business expenses you can--but keep the receipts to support every deduction.

When Applying for a Loan

When you need to borrow money to expand your business, a lender must ensure you can repay your loan. This means they will want to go over your financials with a fine-toothed comb. If your books aren't in order, they'll assume the worst.

In 2022, I spoke with a colleague of mine about a real estate investor client who was trying to get a loan to buy an investment property. Unfortunately, the investor's books were not in good order, and the lender couldn't make sense of his finances. The gentleman got turned down for the loan.

The client went back to the drawing board and hired a bookkeeper to organize and fix the bookkeeping. He eventually got his books in order and went back to the lender. But by then, interest rates had gone from around 4 percent to above 6 percent. The investor got the loan, but the interest on that million-dollar loan went from $40,000 to $60,000 per year.

The lesson: Because the client was not organized ahead of time and did not value good bookkeeping, it cost him dearly. It cost him an additional $20,000 a year in interest. But the interest expense was just the tip of the iceberg. This $20,000 a year expense is every year for the life of the loan. He then has the compounding opportunity cost of what that interest expense could do for him and his family for the rest if his life and the rest of their life. That $20,000 would have created more value had it gone toward paying off debt, buying more income-producing assets, or being put toward the *Family Banking System*.

I've seen other disorganized business owners and investors who are not prepared to take advantage of opportunities when they arise and, hence, lose out on huge opportunities. It happens all the time. It's important to always be ready when opportunities present themselves.

Segregate Your Accounts

Business owners must have a separate set of books and a separate account for every business enterprise. Ideally, you want separate credit cards for each business as well. Separate books and accounts provide several benefits: By keeping separate accounts, you'll accurately track income and expenses for each business and avoid commingling funds. This also makes tax preparation much easier, less time-consuming and expensive, and reduces the risk of error.

Categorizing your business transactions from a single business entity within a single bank account, and *only and exclusively* within that single bank account, makes life easier, with all money coming in as income and all money going out as either expense or distribution. Meanwhile, the failure to keep a strict separation between each business entity—and between your businesses and your own personal finances—carries some significant potential consequences. The IRS hates comingling of funds it and it erases the corporate veil, which is already thin because you're a closely held corporation. This jeopardizes your limited liability protection and makes it difficult or impossible to contain liability within the entity. Failure to segregate your business from your personal assets and your business accounts from each other potentially puts everything you own at risk.

Chapter 2
Entity Structure

The structure of your business is the second-most important tax strategy. Your entity structure dictates what tax benefits you are eligible for. But taxes are only one of the reasons your business structure is important. The structure of your business is vital for asset protection, estate planning, and succession planning.

I am not going to go deep into this subject matter. I could write an entire book on this subject alone. They each have their pros and cons. If I were to chose one entity structure to never be a part of, it would be a partnership. I want to note this is in no way advice.

Partnerships have too many tax issues and too many liability issues. I highly recommend speaking with an educated tax advisor and attorney before entering into a partnership. In my opinion, there are better ways to structure a business with multiple owners.

There are multiple ways to structure your business:

- Sole Proprietorship
- Single Member LLC
- Multi-Member LLC
- S Corporation
- C Corporation
- Partnership
- General Partnership
- General Limited Partnership
- Unlimited Partnership
- Public Limited Company
- Holding Company (also known as Parent Company)
- Subsidiary Company (owned by a Holding Company)

Legal *vs.* Tax Structures

Your legal structure and tax structure are two different aspects of your business that should not be considered separately. Your legal structure refers to how your business is legally organized, such as a sole proprietor, partnership, LLC, or corporation. It dictates how your business operates under the law.

The tax structure, on the other hand, refers to how the government taxes the business. This can include how income is reported, how deductions are taken, how taxes are paid, and what tax strategies apply to your business. While your legal and tax structures are separate, they impact each other in significant ways. If your legal documents don't match your tax documents, the risk of failing an audit will increase. Inconsistencies between the two can raise red flags when you file your taxes and during an audit.

For example, suppose your legal documents indicate you're operating as a corporation, but your tax documents indicate you are a sole proprietor. In that case, the IRS may question the accuracy of your bookkeeping and your tax return and request additional documentation to support your filing. Or suppose you're filing as an S-Corp, but you're not taking payroll.

Inconsistencies between your legal and tax documents will likely lead to additional questions and scrutiny from the IRS during an audit. To avoid potential issues during an audit, it's vital to ensure that your legal and tax documents are consistent and accurate.

As a business owner, you have the responsibility to maintain asset protection and to follow corporate protocols and procedures. More and more LLCs are being pierced, and owners are being found personally liable because their LLCs were not formed correctly, and corporate protocols and procedures were not followed.

Piercing the Corporate Veil

The primary advantage of being incorporated in business is that 'you're not held personally liable for the debts or liabilities of the entity. In other words, creditors can only pursue the 'entity's assets and cannot reach your personal assets. This layer of protection separating the entity's liabilities from the business owner's assets is commonly known as the **corporate veil**. If you don't maintain the shield of protection, it's possible a creditor can pierce the corporate veil and reach your personal assets. Laws differ from state to state, but there are several reasons why the corporate veil might be pierced.

There might be a failure to maintain separate corporate records, minutes, and statuses. Furthermore, operating a business as a corporation means strict adherence to corporate formalities. This includes holding annual meetings, documenting minutes and resolutions, appointing officers, directors, and managers, filing tax returns properly, and following rules specified in corporate documents. It could also be due to not using the proper company name in your operations or documents or allowing the commingling of funds. You must have a clear separation between the company's financial operations and your personal financial affairs.

There should be a separation between personal assets and business assets. You should have a complete formation of the company with all the supporting documents.

- Hold annual meetings and record them in a corporate book.
- Renew your entity with the proper Secretary of State.
- File your taxes properly.
- Create a business entity.
- Maintain your corporate veil.
- Use proper contracts and procedures.
- Purchase the correct business insurance.
- Purchase an umbrella insurance policy.
- Proper formation documents.
- Maintain an up-to-date operating agreement.

S-Corporation and C-Corporations can provide you with some amazing benefits, but if you don't maintain your business properly, you can have a lot of unexpected problems.

Do You Have Multiple Businesses?

One of the challenges is figuring out the most effective way to structure each business. Should you integrate trusts and corporations into your structure? Most likely. Should you integrate holding companies into your structure? Possibly. If you own real estate, perhaps a good idea is to separate the real estate into one business and the operation or management of those properties into another.

If you have multiple business, perhaps a C-Corporation owning all the other businesses is a good idea.

One big mistake real estate investors make is running all their real estate through a single entity. That is, they use the same business to flip properties as they do to hold their long-term rentals. Long-term rentals have different tax rules than flips. Short-term rentals have different tax rules as well.

If your business brings in revenue from multiple sources, it may be beneficial to split your business into multiple businesses. Here are a few examples:

Let's say you own a chiropractic business or a dentist's office. You sell supplements or other supplies. It could benefit you to separate the chiropractic clinic from the business that sells supplements. You may be able to classify the supplements as passive income, which could have better tax benefits.

Let's pretend, for a moment, that you own your office building. It may benefit you to create a separate LLC to hold the real estate and have your business pay the other LLC the rental income from the property you own. You may be able to pay yourself a lower salary from that LLC than you do from the chiropractic practice. This technique can reduce your self-employment tax liability because rent from your real estate business and rental income are not subject to self-employment tax.

Suppose you have multiple businesses. Perhaps you want to have a separate marketing business that does the marketing for all your businesses. You can also have a separate company that does all your payroll human resources for all the businesses. This company in turn charges the other companies for its service and their payroll costs, plus a profit.

Re-categorize Your Income

As a business owner, you have many opportunities to re-categorize income and pay less in taxes. The first thing you need to do is maximize your income while minimizing taxes. For that, you need to understand that income is taxed as a regular income-tax rate, a capital gains rate, or as a dividend rate. On most occasions, you can change how part of your income is taxed simply by reallocating how your money is earned. Moreover, you can also achieve this by shifting your income to a lower bracket.

But you must remember: All tax planning must have a business purpose other than reducing taxes.

Common Small Business Entities

Most business owners start as sole proprietors. As they grow, they establish a limited liability company (LLC) or corporation to help protect them from liability. They believe an LLC will save them on their taxes. I want to be clear about this: an LLC is a *legal* entity. It has nothing to do with taxes. Once you transition from a sole proprietorship to an LLC, you must choose how you want to be taxed. You may choose to continue being taxed as a sole proprietor (disregarded entity), an S corporation, or a C corporation.

As an S corporation, you are considered both a business owner **AND** an employee of the business, and you must pay yourself a salary. The income you receive from your S-Corporation is considered either, salary or distributions. One of the unique aspects of S corps is the ability to split income into two parts: salary and distributions. *Salary* is the amount of money a business owner pays themselves for the work they do as an employee of the corporation. This income is reported on Form W2 and is subject to self-employment taxes. *Distributions* are payments from company profits made to the business owner, not subject to employment taxes.

It would be fantastic if a business owner could pay 99 percent of their income as distributions and pay no self-employment tax. But that's not possible. The IRS requires business owners to pay themselves a "reasonable" salary for the work they do as employees of the corporation. This means that, you *must* be on payroll and receive regular paychecks, which is similar to working for someone else. Setting up your payroll procedure is the most critical aspect of owning and operating an S corporation to save taxes.

There is an art to determining the most efficient salary. Some business owners may make the mistake of either paying themselves too much salary or not paying themselves enough. Paying yourself less salary can reduce your FICA tax, especially if you are under the social security wage base. On the other hand, not paying yourself enough salary can prevent you from taking advantage of other tax-reducing strategies. It is essential to carefully consider the appropriate compensation to pay yourself when operating an S corporation to ensure compliance with IRS rules and maximize the tax benefits of this business structure.

Factors to consider when determining a "reasonable salary," according to the IRS and tax court courses, include the following:

- Training and experience
- Duties and responsibilities
- Time and effort devoted to the business
- Dividend history (shareholder distributions)
- Payments to non-shareholder employees
- Timing and manner of paying bonuses to key people
- Compensation by comparable businesses for similar services
- Compensation agreements
- Use of a formula to determine compensation

Determining the ideal salary that will make the IRS happy *and* maximize your tax savings can be difficult. To determine the most advantageous salary, it is recommended to work with a firm that will analyze your business using a questionnaire, IRS criteria, court rulings, geographic data, and their wage database.

I see many business owners trying to do payroll themselves. Don't! Hire someone. The IRS is not forgiving if you screw up payroll. I would much rather face them on income tax issues than payroll issues. Paying yourself incorrectly, such as using a 1099 instead of a Form W-2, can result in significant tax liabilities, interest, and penalties. A payroll service can help ease the payroll process and ensure that all necessary withholdings and filings are correctly made. The penalty for screwing up these taxes can be severe. I do not recommend doing your own payroll.

The LLC Salary Mistake

I see many business owners trying to take a salary from a single-member LLC. However, the IRS clearly states that an active business owner cannot take a salary from a single-member LLC, or an LLC taxed as a partnership. As an LLC, all the revenue passes through the business onto your 1040 and is taxed the same. You can, however, take a salary as an owner-employee of an LLC taxed as an S Corporation.

C Corporations *vs.* S Corporations

If you anticipate reinvesting operating profits back into the business rather than paying them out as distributions to owners, a C Corporation may be a better option than an S Corporation.

C Corporations and Double Taxation

Oftentimes, you'll hear, "DOUBLE TAXATION! Don't choose a C corporation!" And it is true that there's an issue with C corporations. This is because unlike S corporations, where distributions "flow through" directly to your income tax return without taxation at the corporate level, all C corporations must pay corporate income tax on their profits before distributing dividends to shareholders. And then, shareholders must pay taxes again on these dividends on their personal income tax returns.

For most small business owners, it does not make sense to be structured as a C corporation. But C corporations certainly have their place! If you have multiple businesses, it may make sense to have one business structured as a C corporation because there are some tax strategies available to them that are not available to other entities.

A C-Corporation may be a good option when it's at the top of your entity structure hierarchy. It may be a good option when you have multiple businesses and want to use specific tax strategies. It may be a good option when you have multiple "owners."

If you eventually want to take your company public, you'll need a C corporation to issue common stock to shareholders over the stock exchanges and raise money. A C corporation can also be a good choice if you plan on reinvesting your earnings right back into your company rather than paying them out as distributions. If you're not paying distributions, the double taxation issue for C corporations is irrelevant.

Choosing the correct business entity is only half the battle. Once you select the correct entity, you must also follow the rules. Your tax documents must match your legal paperwork.

Holding Company

A holding company is a business entity, such as a corporation, LLC, or limited partnership, that exists to hold assets. It can hold stocks, intellectual property, real estate, or other companies.

A holding company doesn't do anything other than exercise control over the management of the company. Warren Buffett's Berkshire Hathaway is a famous and fabulously successful example of a holding company.

A holding company may allow you more control over the timing of compensation. It can effectively allow you to retain income inside the holding company until a later point in time when you are ready to receive the income.

This business structure allows a business's profits to flow tax-free to the owner via dividends and can be retained in the holding company until the business owner needs the money personally. The dividend paid to the holding company does not create a tax liability for the business owner.

It may also be beneficial to hold certain assets inside a holding company for federal estate tax planning purposes. Any assets you own in your name when you die may be subject to federal estate tax, depending on the value of your estate.

Separation and Limited Liability

A holding company allows a separation of ownership between your businesses and your own personal assets.

For example, let's say you own an accounting firm and an office building. You could create an LLC as a holding company that owns the building. You could create a second LLC for the operating company that manages the building. You could create another LLC for the accounting firm.

Someone with a claim against the accounting firm could not seize the building, or vice versa. Holding companies and operating company arrangements can reduce self-employment taxes or payroll taxes.

Your income from your accounting firm is earned income, and you have self-employment tax and income taxes to pay on the earned income. However, you can reduce your earned income by the amount of your rental expenses.

The rental income is considered passive and only taxed at the income tax level. Of course, you must have a lease, and the rent must be at market rates. You cannot charge an exuberant rent rate just to save some money on self-employment taxes. The IRS could charge you penalties and interest in addition to income taxes and self-employment.

Holding companies may also be used for other purposes, including mergers and acquisitions and the eventual sale of the firm. The holding company allows you to maintain a separation of ownership. There are many reasons to have a separation of ownership, including tax advantages and risk-management advantages. Let's say you have a business partner in the accounting firm. You may not want your partner to have ownership in the building, so you separate the businesses from one another.

Chapter 3
Basic Tax Strategies You Should be Aware of

Accountable Plans

An accountable plan is the most basic tax strategy for your S Corporation, and every S corporation should have one. If you have an S Corporation, but do not have an accountable plan, I guarantee you're overpaying taxes. Why is your tax professional not talking to you about a basic strategy? Probably because they know nothing about it. What else do they not know? It's time to hire a tax strategist!

An *accountable plan* enables an employer to reimburse employees for business expenses *without the reimbursements being considered taxable income to the worker*. An accountable plan also enables owner-employees to be reimbursed for expenses paid out of pocket. The expenses become deductions for the business, and the employee or employee-owner can be reimbursed, creating a nontaxable income for these individuals.

Reimbursements under an accountable plan are neither subject to withholding taxes nor must they be included on W-2 forms, as they are not considered additional compensation. To qualify as an accountable plan, the arrangement must meet certain requirements set by the IRS, which are outlined below.

- Business connection
- Substantiation (expense reports with receipts)
- No excess payments
- Reimbursed in a timely manner.

If you make payments to employees that are not subject to an accountable plan, the IRS could consider these payments as additional wages. Examples of possible payments include payments for mileage, home office, travel, and meals.

Note: If you have a C Corporation or an LLC taxed as an S Corporation, you must have an accountable plan in place to reimburse yourself for the business use of your home office. Your business does not get to write off your home office

Automobiles and Taxes

A common question I hear is, "What strategy is best for me with my car, truck, SUV, or RV? Should I use the mileage or the actual method? Should I lease or buy new or used?" Should I write it all off this year?"

And the answer is always this: *It depends!*

The business use of vehicles falls under four basic circumstances:

- You own the vehicle, but your business reimburses you for the use of it by the mile.
- You own the vehicle, and you take a mileage deduction.
- You own the vehicle, and you lease it back to the business.
- The business owns the vehicle, not you, and it's titled in the business's name.

This includes SUVs, trucks, RVs, motorcycles, and more. And yes, it's possible to use an RV or even a boat to reduce your taxes. BUT do not get greedy. These can be red flags if not reported correctly.

Most of our clients use one of two main options: The mileage *method*, or the *actual expenditure method*.

The Mileage Method

This is a fixed deduction amount that you can take for every business mile you drive your vehicle for business. It includes everything you might pay for with your car, such as fuel, repairs, maintenance, auto payments, etc., except interest on an auto loan. You can take the mileage deduction AND the interest deduction. This is a common expense I see missing on tax returns when I review them.

The Actual Expenditure Method

This allows the business owner to take all the expenses listed above *plus depreciation*. However, it requires you to keep excellent records.

To make things a little easier for you, I've listed a few guidelines that may help you choose the best strategy for your situation. Remember, these are nothing more than guidelines. Without looking at other parts of your tax plan, the best strategy cannot be determined.

Business Use of Vehicle Guidelines

- If you are going to put on a lot of business miles, and the car is relatively inexpensive, then the mileage method may be beneficial.
- If you're not going to use the vehicle very much for business, and it's an average-cost vehicle used exclusively or primarily for business (meaning 50 percent business use or more), then the actual method may be beneficial.

- If you're not going to have a lot of business miles and it's a more expensive car used exclusively or primarily for business (again, meaning 50 percent business use or more), leasing and the actual method may be beneficial. You'll have lower monthly payments, making this a better economic decision and a much better write-off than the mileage method.
- If you expect to have low miles and use a lower-cost vehicle, and your business use of the vehicle will be less than 50 percent, you're going to be stuck with the mileage method because you don't qualify for the actual method.
- If you have an extra car in the household, driven occasionally by you or other family members for business, you will typically use the mileage method because the business-use percentage will likely be under 50 percent, and that's your only option.
- If you are going to buy a 6,000-pound or more SUV or truck, the actual method may be beneficial for several reasons. First, bonus depreciation is going to be huge. You can immediately deduct up to 80 percent of the business use value of the vehicle (business use percentage times the purchase price). Also, you will likely have a lower MPG, pushing up your actual costs with higher fuel expenses.

If you have a vehicle that gets good gas mileage-such as a hybrid or electric car- but still have average use and miles, the mileage method may be beneficial. The main reasons are:

1) Your operating costs are going to be much lower than those of an average gas vehicle.
2) You don't have to worry about your business use percentage since you're going with mileage, and
3) Hopefully, you can qualify for the clean vehicle tax credit on top of your mileage deduction!

Remember, these are just general guidelines. You need to consider all the facts pertaining to your situation and meet with your tax advisor before choosing a strategy.

A few Tax-Efficient ways to Donate Money

Charitable Lead Trusts

Do you like to give money to charity? The most common way to give money to charity is to write a check. The problem with writing a check is that you're giving money that's already been taxed. A better way is to give away money that has not been taxed.

A *Charitable Lead Trust* is an irrevocable trust designed to provide financial support to one or more charities for a period of time, with the remaining assets eventually going to family members or other beneficiaries.

It can potentially provide tax benefits, such as income-tax deductions and estate or gift tax savings.

How Charitable Lead Trusts Work

1) **Contribute to fund the trust.** The grantor, or person establishing the charitable lead trust, contributes to fund the trust, which is set up to operate for a fixed term, such as a set number of years or the life of one or more people. Assets such as publicly traded stock, real estate, private business interests, and private company stock may be contributed.
2) **Payments are sent to the charity.** Payments from the trust are disbursed to the selected charity or charities as either a fixed annuity payment or a percentage of the trust.
3) **Distribute to non-charitable beneficiaries.**

Once the term of the charitable lead trust ends, the principal is distributed to you or the other designated beneficiaries in a manner that can minimize or even eliminate transfer taxes.

Charitable Remainder Trust

A charitable remainder trust (CRT) is a tax-efficient way for individuals to donate to a charitable organization while also providing income for themselves or their beneficiaries. This type of trust allows the donor to transfer assets, such as cash or stocks, into the trust, receive an immediate tax deduction, and then receive income from the trust for a specified number of years or the rest of his or her life. After the specified period, the remaining assets in the trust are distributed to the designated charitable organization.

If structured correctly, the tax savings of a charitable lead trust can outweigh the amount you give away. People usually create them to avoid tax on appreciated assets. That's because the trust can do something you can't—it can sell appreciated assets without paying tax on the capital gain.

How Charitable Remainder Trusts Work

1) **Transfer property.** Transfer real estate or a business to a trust and designate a charitable organization to receive the remaining assets after the specified period.
2) **Let the trust sell it.** After that, the trust will pay you income from the trust for the remainder of your life.
3) **Donate.** The remainder after your death goes to the tax-exempt charity organization of your choice.

Donor-Advised Funds

A *donor-advised fund* is a philanthropic giving vehicle that allows individuals, families, or organizations to make tax-deductible contributions to a fund administered by a sponsoring organization, such as a community foundation or a financial institution. The donor can then recommend grants to eligible charitable organizations from the fund over time.

Key Elements

Contributions to donor-advised funds are generally tax-deductible in the year they are made, subject to certain limitations, and donors should maintain accurate records and seek guidance from tax professionals. While donors can recommend grants, the sponsoring organization holds legal authority to approve or disapprove, and IRS regulations mandate annual qualifying distributions, usually at least 5 percent of the fund's average net assets, with investment income within the fund being tax-exempt for potential growth.

Implementation

1. **Establishing a DAF.** Individuals or entities can set up a DAF through a sponsoring organization, such as a community foundation, a public charity, or a financial institution. The process typically involves opening an account and making an initial tax-deductible contribution to the fund.
2. **Simplified Record-Keeping.** DAFs simplify the administrative burdens of charitable giving. Donors make one tax-deductible contribution to their DAF and then recommend grants to multiple charities, streamlining record-keeping.

Delaware Statutory Trusts

A *Delaware Statutory Trust* (DST) is a type of trust created under the laws of the state of Delaware. It can be used for a variety of purposes, including real estate and investments. A DST provides flexibility in terms of asset ownership, and management can have multiple beneficiaries, which allows for the pooling of resources and management of assets among multiple investors.

This can make it easier for small investors to participate in larger investment opportunities that they otherwise would not have the opportunity to invest in. This is because the assets are held in a trust that protects them from the beneficiary's creditors.

Benefits of Delaware Statutory Trusts

- **Tax efficiency.** DSTs can be structured to minimize or even eliminate certain taxes, such as capital gains tax, which can help maximize returns.
- DSTs can also provide a tax benefit to investors, such as the ability to pass incoming deductions on to the beneficiary of the trust.
- **Estate planning.** DSTs allow you to transfer assets directly to future generations. Because the assets are held in trust, they bypass probate. They are governed under the laws of the state of Delaware, which is generally considered a favorable jurisdiction for trusts and other business entities.
- **Anonymity.** DSTs can be set up so that the beneficiaries of the trusts are not publicly disclosed. This provides privacy and confidentiality for the investors.
- **Diversification.** DSTs allow investors to diversify their portfolios by investing in a variety of assets, such as real estate, private equity, and other alternative investments.
- **Liquidity.** DSTs can provide liquidity for investors since they can be bought and sold on the secondary market.

DEPRECIATION as a Tax Strategy

Depreciation is an accounting method that allows a business owner to spread out the cost of a tangible asset over its useful life. Bonus depreciation is the most popular and a great option. But what happens if the Bonus Depreciation goes away? I want to make you aware of some of the options available. There are various types of depreciation, including:

- Declining balance
- Accelerated depreciation
- Double-declining balance
- Straight-line method
- Bonus depreciation

Be intentional in how you depreciate your equipment, vehicles, and other assets. Just because you are legally able to depreciate equipment or a vehicle in one year, you should. When we decide the best depreciation strategy, we take into consideration:

- all your income and the timing of that income
- all your planned financial transactions, including the timing of taking income or selling other assets
- the immediate and near-future financial needs of the business; and which option will provide greater benefits.

Depreciation Recapture

We also consider the effect *depreciation recapture* may have on your taxes. The biggest tax bill for many real estate investors arrives when they sell their properties. I often see depreciation recapture either forgotten, or not taken into consideration when selling an asset.

Depreciation recapture is the portion of your gain attributed to the depreciation you took on the property during your ownership. Depreciation recapture is generally taxed as ordinary income at a maximum rate of 25 percent.

Little details like this can make a difference when choosing between closing on a property on December 31st or January 1st. Now, of course, many investors utilize a 1031 exchange to avoid this problem, but a 1031 exchange is kicking the tax bucket down the road.

Family Board of Directors

A Family Board of Directors is a strategic framework for involving family members in critical business and financial decisions. By making family members part of your business venture, you can utilize other tax strategies and deductions you may not otherwise be able to use.

Qualifications

The concept of a Family Board of Directors is applicable to businesses of all sizes. It holds significance not only as a tax and legal strategy but also as a vital business strategy for long-term success.

Key Elements

Establish a "Board of Advisors" in the Operating Agreement for LLCs, applicable to partnerships and sole proprietorships, while using a "Board of Directors" for S Corporations to formalize decision-making. Leverage tax benefits through deductible expenses in regular board meetings, clarify compensation for members, offer educational resources, enhance asset protection, involve family members for tax benefits, and use a structured approach for decision-making and conflict resolution.

Implementation Steps

- Forming the Board
- Designation. Select board members during entity formation or at any time, even
- during annual meetings.
- Documentation. Document the process as "minutes" and have members sign to
- confirm their willingness to serve.
- Record keeping. Keep comprehensive records of meetings, decisions, and
- actions taken for transparency and accountability.

Family Office Management

For a family wealth-planning structure that is more active than most, you can establish a family office management company. This entity will contract with the various family holding companies and operating businesses.

Income from the management contracts is revenue to the management company. This revenue, in turn, can be converted into salaries, benefits, and business expenses for family members in various tax brackets.

With some careful planning, expenses and deductions can potentially be allocated to family members in high tax brackets, while income can be allocated to family members in low tax brackets.

Annual Meetings

Corporations are required to hold member, shareholder, and board meetings. These meetings incur expenses, which are tax deductible. Board meetings in resort locations can be deductible if you explain:

1) the business purpose served by the location, and
2) why the board could not meet at the business's primary location.

For example, a special location could entice the board members to attend, take good notes, and document the results of the meeting.

Note: Making sure that your travel has a "business purpose" is critical. Even properly planned holiday travel can generate a significant tax deduction. This can include visiting family or going to our special/romantic locations around the U.S. or the world. To claim this deduction, however, you must follow some rules.

If you have a corporation, the travel could be for a meeting of your shareholders or board of directors. If you have an LLC, elect a board of advisors to assist the manager or managers of the company. This is an excellent opportunity to discuss the operations of the company over the past year, such as profits, losses, acquisitions, new ventures, and goal setting. Use the advice of your board members and make plans for the next year. Travel expenses are 100 percent deductible when traveling for business, meaning you may write off travel expenses. These include expenses for the following:

- airfare
- hotel and Airbnb
- rental cars, Uber, and Lyft
- valets and taxis
- trains, tolls, etc.

The "Augusta Rule"

This rule is named after Augusta, Georgia, where the Masters Golf Tournament is held each year. Homeowners in Augusta may rent their homes to people attending the tournament from out of town for up to fourteen days and **pay no taxes on the income**. But the same principle applies to other events, such as the Super Bowl, the Olympics, and similar events that draw tens of thousands of people to a city.

As a business owner, you can *rent your personal residence to your business* and receive the same benefit. To take advantage of the tax benefits of the Augusta Rule, the business owner must be the owner of the residence being rented, and the residence must be in the United States.

To qualify for the tax benefits of the Augusta Rule, the rental must not be used for entertainment or recreation. Many occasions can be hosted at the residence, however, such as annual shareholder and director meetings or off-site employee retreats.

The **BUSINESS** must pay a fair market value for the rental, which you can determine by researching comparable rentals on websites such as Airbnb or Zillow or by contacting local meeting venues to find out what they charge for similar spaces.

And that rental fee for up to two weeks is *tax-deductible* to the business and *tax-free* to you!

The Augusta Rule only applies to the rental of a primary residence or vacation home and does not apply to the rental of other types of properties.

Additionally, to take advantage of the tax benefits of the Augusta Rule, the business must be a separate legal entity from the owner of the residence. A sole proprietorship—in which the business and the owner are considered the same for tax purposes—is not eligible for the tax benefit under the Augusta Rule.

Hire Children and Grandparents

Utilizing your family to reduce your taxes is a great benefit for all. Hiring your children can be a great way to cut taxes on your income by shifting it to someone in a lower tax bracket. For example, if you're in the 36 percent tax bracket and your child is in the 10 percent tax bracket, it can make terrific sense to hire your own child.

This gets income off your own income tax return and onto your child's—and at a much lower tax bracket! The kids would then use this money to save, invest, or spend. Not only do you receive a tax break, but your kids earn money, learn valuable skills, and (hopefully!) learn the value of a dollar in the process. There are no clear-cut rules regarding how old your kids must be to work for you. But there is an unspoken rule: If your children are under the age of seven, it's a red flag for the IRS.

Note: You must pay them a *reasonable* wage for the services they perform. The tax court says a *reasonable wage* is what you'd pay an employee for the same service. Meaning you can't just pay them double or triple the going rate. These services can include videography, social media management, editing, shredding, administrative work, answering phones, and so on. Hiring children is a great way to let your kids earn money, shift income to them, and let them pay for their own activities.

Be sure to specify job descriptions and keep timesheets. Don't pay in cash. Pay by check or electronically, so you can document the payment. You must deposit payroll checks into an account in the *child's* name. This can be a bank account or a Roth IRA.

As parents, we are required to spend a certain amount of money on our kids to take care of them. We need to buy them food, clothing and shelter. However, summer camps and fees for special classes such as dancing, piano lessons, sports, etc are not obligations of parental support. Let's say your son wants to go to a wrestling or football camp. Instead of you paying for it, with the money you earn and are taxed on, your son can work for you and earn the money himself.

Right now, you are paying these expenses with after-taxed dollars. They are going to do these activities anyway, you might as well pay for these activities with untaxed money!

Hire Your Parents

Another way to make good use of tax brackets is to involve your parents. If your parents are in a lower tax bracket, it may be beneficial to hire them or give part of your business or real estate to them. This can reduce your taxable income and shift your income to a lower tax bracket. Here's how it works:

You give a portion of your limited partnership as a corporation or LLC to your parents. Any income from their share of the business flows through their income tax return, and it's taxed at their rate.

You remain the manager of the LLC, the majority stockholder of S Corp., or the general partner of the limited partnership. You remain in control. If you are careful about how much you give them, then you won't have any gift tax. Moreover, you can also hire them as employees and shift some of the income to their tax bracket.

Bonus: If your parents (or in-laws) die before you and bequeath the assets back to you, you get the benefit of a stepped-up basis. That means your capital gains on the asset—if any—restart at zero. Not at whatever the appreciation is since you originally bought it. This benefit alone can save many, many thousands of dollars in taxes for those who are patient.

Dividing Ownership

You can also divide ownership of a business among your family members and save a lot of money. This is another way we use the tax brackets to our advantage.

Example: If you have a business that makes $387,000 a year and you have five children, you can split that income into seven parts. If you and your spouse remain the sole owners and pay the tax on the entire $387,000, you would pay more because it's in a higher tax bracket. You would also pay unemployment and social security taxes. You would also pay an additional 3.8 percent tax on net investment income on much of that income, courtesy of the Affordable Care Act.

But by dividing the ownership interest between you and your children, you can potentially split that income into six or seven parts. So instead of everything being under your tax return, taxed at 36 percent plus state taxes, every dollar would now be taxed at perhaps 12 percent—provided you structure the strategy properly!

If you structure your divided ownership properly through the correct trusts and entities, you maintain control over the business.

Section 105: Medical Reimbursement Plans

Do you know your business can pay for your kid's braces? That's right; your business can pay for medical expenses pre-tax.

The Section 105 plan is an "employee" benefit plan. To qualify for this plan, one must be an employee. If, however, your business is a sole proprietorship (which includes a single-member LLC), a partnership, or an S corporation, then you're considered self-employed, and you do not qualify for this tax strategy. This tax strategy is best suited for C-Corporations. In this scenario, you can't get benefits from the plan, so you must figure out another way to qualify.

Here are some ways to reduce your taxes on medical expenditures:

Hire your spouse: If you're a sole proprietor (or a single-member LLC taxed as a proprietorship) and you're married, you may hire your spouse to cover that medical expense. If you are a partner or are involved in a partnership, you can hire your spouse—provided your spouse does not own more than 5 percent of the business.

Segregate your income: If you're a shareholder or a member of an entity taxed as an S corporation, neither you nor your spouse will qualify for the medical plan. If it's possible, segregate a part of your income into a separate entity. That way, you can run the plan through that entity.

Use a Section 105 plan for family members. Let's say you're a parent working as a real estate agent. You have the option to hire your teenage child and use the plan to pay for their glasses, braces, or other qualified medical expenses.

You can even hire your retired parents to help cover their medical costs. If you qualify, the plan lets you reimburse your employees and their spouses (YOU) and dependents (YOUR KIDS) for all their medical expenses. You'll even avoid paying self-employment tax on the money you deduct through the 105 plan.

What can you deduct under a Section 105 Plan?

Copays	Insurance Deductibles	Vasectomy	Acupuncture
Lab fees	Dental	OBGYN costs	Speech therapy
Sleep aids	Vaccinations	Infertility treatment	Medical operations
Physical therapy	Orthodontic fees	Contacts and Glasses	Eye drops
X-rays	Prescriptions	Flu shots	Certain Supplements
Prescriptions	Psychiatrist fees	Allergy Pills	Chiropractic

Other Health Plans

Health Savings Accounts (HSAs). A health savings account is a medical savings account for taxpayers that has a high deductible. This account can grow tax-deferred, like an IRA. Contributions are tax-deductible, and qualified distributions are tax-free. Unlike a flexible spending account, an HSA does not go to zero at the end of each year, and unused contributions can be continually rolled over to help fund retirement. Most financial advisors do not recommend these financial tools because they cannot make money from them.

Qualified Small Employer Health Reimbursement Arrangements (QSEHRAs). (pronounced "Cue Sarah). A QSEHRA is a qualified small employer health reimbursement arrangement. It is a company-funded account that allows for reimbursement of medical expenses. It's only available to businesses with fewer than fifty full-time equivalents that *do not* sponsor a group health insurance benefit of their own.

The QSEHRA typically reimburses employees for premiums they pay for their own individual health insurance coverage. To receive a QSEHRA benefit, the employee must purchase an ACA-qualified health insurance plan.

This reimbursement can be considered part of the employee's compensation package. So it is tax-deductible for the business as a compensation expense. However, benefits paid to employees within a health reimbursement arrangement are tax-free.

Note: This makes a QSEHRA more tax-efficient than simply paying them a cash stipend to buy health insurance or reimburse them for health insurance premiums. These methods would be fully taxable to the employee and generate a social security tax liability for both of you.

Reimbursements are flexible and have a maximum contribution amount. As of 2024, the maximum QSEHRA contribution for employees with individual coverage is $5,850, and $11,800 for employees with family coverage.

IRC Section 401(h) Plans. This is a retirement plan with a medically focused bonus. The account is attached to a cash balance plan (or defined benefit plan) that is offered by the employer. It is funded with pre-tax dollars, grows tax-deferred, allows for tax-free qualified withdrawals, and allows for tax bracket-shifting opportunities.

- Pre-tax contributions, if applicable, reduce your taxable income.
- Tax-free distributions, including earnings, for qualifying medical expenses.

Oil and Gas

Investing in oil and gas involves directing funds toward activities related to the exploration, extraction, refining, or distribution of oil and natural gas.

You can anticipate saving anywhere between 40 and 80 percent of the amount that you invest. For example, if you contribute $100,000, you can deduct $40,000 to $80,000 off of your income.

And depending on which tax bracket you're in, this can be thousands of dollars in taxes that you save. The second benefit is the return on your investment. These funds typically return anywhere between 15 percent and higher returns over the course of the year, and you should recoup your initial investment within three to four years.

Now there's a variety of funds to choose from, and depending on what your goals and objectives are, it's important that you talk with an advisor who understands oil and gas and your tax strategist to make sure that you're picking the one that's best for you.

Benefits

Investments in oil and gas offer significant tax benefits, including deductions for exploration and development costs as well as the deferral of taxes on earnings until the resource is eventually sold.

An investment in oil and gas is available for anyone who wants to reduce their tax liability. Most funds are designed for the taxpayer to be a general partner in the first year, so this allows a deduction against most types of income.

Tax Savings

The exact tax benefits vary depending on the fund. The anticipated deductions range between 50 percent and 80% of the amount invested. For example, if $100k is invested, the anticipated deduction would be between $50,000 and $80,000.

These deductions can be used to offset a wide range of income types from elsewhere in your overall portfolio, including:

- W2
- Sale of a Business
- Roth Conversion
- Required Minimum Distributions (RMDs),
- Being an alternative to a 1031 Exchange

- Stock Options
- Net Unrealized Appreciation (NUA), and Medicare Surplus/Net Investment Income Tax.

Diversification

Investing in oil, which is not tied to conventional assets like stocks and bonds, aids in portfolio diversification. Additionally, it serves as a hedge against inflation, given that oil prices frequently increase in tandem with inflationary trends.

Investment Returns

Should they well achieve production objectives and generate the anticipated total output, investors have the potential to realize significant returns through the sale of oil or gas in the competitive open market.

Oil and Gas Deductions

Intangible Drilling Costs (IDCs) can be fully deducted in the first year of the investment, reducing your taxable income and increasing cash flow early in the investment cycle.

Costs incurred in the drilling process that cannot be easily quantified or physically seen, such as labor, drilling mud, and chemicals.

Depletion Allowance

This is a tax deduction for the decrease in the value of an oil or gas deposit as it is produced. It allows investors to recover the cost of their investment over time.

Bonus Depreciation

Allows investors to deduct a percentage of the total investment cost in the first year of the investment.

Passive Loss Deductions

Oil and gas investments are often structured as limited partnerships, or LLCs, which allow investors to offset passive losses from the investment against other passive income.

Tax Credits

The federal government offers various tax credits for investments in alternative energy, including oil and gas.

If you're a real estate investor and are not able to use your losses from your real estate activity against any of your other income, oil and gas may be a saving grace.

If your income exceeds $150,000 a year and you want to offset the losses that your real estate generates through depreciation, you either have to qualify as a real estate professional or through a short-term rental. Qualifying as a real estate professional is very difficult, so here's the workaround:

an investment in oil and gas. The first year you invest in oil and gas, you're considered a general partner, and you'll have the losses that are generated through the depletion and depreciation of the investments. You can use these losses to help offset W-2 income, your business income, and even capital gains tax.

So what happens in Year 2? In Year 2, you're considered a limited partner, and now you're receiving income from this investment, and it's considered to be passive income. So instead of trying to qualify for RE professional status, you have these passive losses that the RE has generated, and now you have this passive income. You can use the passive losses to help offset passive income and, hopefully, just zero out the income from the oil and gas.

Travel Expense Deductions

The IRS allows deductions for business travel for several reasons.

The potential deduction of travel expenses is another benefit of shifting your own business into a family business entity. Here's why:

Travel costs for spouses and children are typically non-deductible. However, if they are involved in the business or have a business-related purpose for traveling, the travel cost can be deductible.

For example, the travel expenses of a child who functions as a videographer for the CEO and travels for that purpose would be deductible. There must, however, be an honest, legitimate, and justifiable reason for the travel.

Note: You can deduct only expenses for days when you are traveling or conducting purposeful work for your company away from your normal place of work. To qualify for the deduction, the employee must work for four hours or more, although weekend expenses can be a write-off because they are sandwiched between workdays.

Four Reasons for A Deductible Trip

1. Annual company meeting

    If you have a corporation, this would be considered your annual meeting of the board of directors and/or shareholders. If you have an LLC, elect a board of advisors to assist the manager or managers of the company. This is an excellent opportunity to discuss the operations of the company over the past year (profits, losses, acquisitions, new ventures, goal-setting, etc.). Your board members should be giving you advice and helping you make plans for next year. Your kids and your spouse could be involved in your business in this capacity.

2. Client visit

    Whenever you travel, ask yourself: Is there a customer or client in the area? Could you cultivate a new relationship or strengthen a current one? Schedule meetings each day you are traveling for at least a few hours and keep notes on what you accomplished and why the meeting was important.

3. Vendor visit

    When traveling, consider whether you could meet with a vendor, supplier, sub-contractor, or affiliate in the town where Grandma or Grandpa live. Could you negotiate new pricing, tour a facility, or talk about networking and how you could work more closely together?

Attend a conference or workshop

Look for relevant workshops in the area you are visiting. These could relate to taxes, legal issues, your business, marketing, websites, SEO, customer relationships, or technical training based on the type of business you have. Perhaps you could visit a local real estate or investment club meeting. The training could be fantastic and justify a great write-off.

4. Check on your rental property

    At least consider and/or attempt to purchase rentals where you typically travel. Could you buy rentals where the extended family lives? You could have family members manage your properties, or you could simply work on the properties while you are visiting.

Pigs get fat, but hogs get slaughtered.

In other words, don't get greedy. With all these strategies, moderation is key. Keep your receipts and records. Make sure that you are doing business each day you aren't traveling, and keep records of what you are doing, who you are meeting with, and how it relates to your business.

Home Administrative Office

Most business owners are familiar with using a home office. Business owners who have a business location outside of their home but also maintain a home administrative office for running the business can claim the home office as their primary office. As a result, all mileage for business purposes from the home office is deductible, including trips to office(s) outside of the home.

Structure Ownership Program (SOP)

A structured ownership program (SOP) is a sophisticated tax strategy designed for individuals and businesses to offset earned income or capital gains during any tax year.

The idea is to segregate income and liabilities among the different LLCs within the series according to the diverse needs of the partners. This allows the majority partner to receive a negative K-1, which can offset his/her other taxable income, whether it be from capital gains or active income.

Write off your Pets.

YES! As a business owner, there are ways to write off your pet expenses. By doing so, you can write off all their expenses, including:

- food
- bedding
- vet bills
- boarding
- grooming supplies

Here are a few ways:

Guard Dog

It's important to keep your property and employees safe. One effective security measure is the use of a guard dog. Simply having a dog that makes noise can be enough. Dogs can detect intruders, and their mere presence can be enough to deter potential threats. They can protect inventory at a warehouse or your equipment from getting stolen.

If your dog legitimately serves a purpose as a guard dog, then you can write it off. As with everything else, you must keep proper documentation and be able to defend your position. You need to indicate how the dog is used for security, whether it's during the day or night, etc. on the tax return list it as "security expense" not "dog expense."

Pest Control

Maintaining a pest-free environment is important for many businesses, especially those in the food service. Cats are one effective method of pest control. They are natural hunters. The IRS recognizes the use of cats as a valid business expense for pest control purposes.

Two famous examples:

Disneyland uses cats for pest control purposes, and in the case of Commissioner *v.* Tellier, the court ruled the costs associated with caring for cats used to control vermin in a junkyard were deductible as a business expense.

Working Animal

Working animals play an important role in many businesses. A few examples include:

- Dogs used for herding livestock
- Rescue dogs at a ski resort
- Police dogs
- Drug sniffing dogs at entrances
- Animals used for therapy
- Horses
- Chickens used to control bugs
- Goats for a yoga business

ADVERTISING

Pets can be great for promoting your business and attracting business. Your pet can be used in videos, print material, logo, signs, website, or your brand. You could bring your pet to event like trade shows or community events. You could also bring your pet into your business or bike shop to greet customers and promote sales.

There are endless opportunities to incorporate your pet into your business brand and experience for your customers. Just legitimize it and keep good records.

DECORATION

You can use aquariums and fish as decorative elements in a business. But they also change the ways employees experience their working space. For an employee to remain productive, he/she must reduce his/her stress.

An aquarium can provide a calming atmosphere and reduce stress levels. Watching fish can lower your heart rate and blood pressure. They are visually appealing for customers and employees and can serve as a branding opportunity.

Chapter 4
SELLING YOUR BUSINESS and TAXES

Stock Sales *vs.* Asset Sales

When you sell a business, you can sell either the stock of the company or the assets of the company. If you sell the stock of your company, you must pay tax at the capital gains rates.

If you sell the assets of your company, most of your gains should be taxed at the capital gain rate if your advisor understands how to negotiate the agreement.

Yes, this means you should have your tax advisor heavily involved in the negotiations when you sell your business. To lower your taxes, your advisor must be involved *before* you sell your business. Usually, business owners and real estate investors end up owing more taxes than they legally had to when they sell their businesses or property because they don't get a tax strategist involved.

I will repeat this: ALWAYS have your tax advisor heavily involved when you sell assets IF you want to be tax efficient.

If you don't care about paying additional taxes, then there's no need to get them involved.

Here are a few examples of some tax consequences that can occur when selling a business or real estate:

1. **Self-employment tax.** If the business owner is financing the sale of a business, it's possible to be subject to self-employment tax on the income resulting from the financing.
2. **Interest income.** The business owner may be subject to taxes on the interest income earned from financing.
3. **Depreciation recapture.** If a business owner claims depreciation on a property, they might be subject to depreciation recapture taxes when they sell the property.
4. **Capital gains tax.** A business owner may be subject to capital gains tax on the sale of property accomplished through owner financing.
5. **State taxes.** State taxes may also apply when selling a property or business. Each state has its own tax laws and rates.

6. **Entity considerations.** Different ownership structures have different tax consequences. This must be considered in your planning.
7. **Debt forgiveness income.** A business owner may be subject to income tax on debt forgiveness income if the buyer is unable to pay the full amount of the loan.

Recasting Your Financials

To get the best price for your business, it's important to show ALL your income and expenses for the last 3 to 5 years. You want to show as much cash flow as possible and you want to make sure it's categorized correctly. Accurate books will help you get more money for your business and will justify a lending institution to lend money to a buyer.

Installment Sales

An installment sale, also known as *seller financing,* is a sale of an asset in which the buyer makes a series of annual payments rather than paying for the property all at once. In this type of transaction, revenue and expenses can be recorded at the time of cash collection rather than at the time of the sale.

When you sell a company or investment property, you may face a large tax bill on the profits. These taxes may be higher than you expect due to your other income.

One way to maximize profits and defer taxes is by using an installment sale. This option may not work for everyone, as you may initially want all the money from the sale at once. An installment sale, however, can leave you with more money in the end.

Advantages of Installment Sales

Installment sales allow the seller to spread out income from the sale of an asset over multiple years. Receiving all the money in one year may force them into a higher tax bracket. This is especially significant for high-income sellers who may be subject to the 3.8 percent net investment income tax.

In an installment sale, the tax on the entire gain is not paid in one year. Only a portion of the gain is taxable in the year of the sale, with the remainder being taxable in the years that payments are received. This can result in lower tax overall liability because the gain from the installment sale is spread out over several years, potentially allowing you to benefit from the tax rate differential in each of those years.

For example, if you arrange a five-year installment sale where $50,000 of the gain is taxed at the 15 percent rate each year instead of the 20 percent rate (if the entire gain had been taxed in the year of sale), you would save $2,500 ($50,000 × 5 percent tax rate differential) each year, for a total savings of $12,500 ($2,500 × 5 years).

These rates, however, may change as the tax law changes.

An installment sale can potentially allow you to stay below the capital gains threshold each year, resulting in no capital gains tax being paid. You can get creative and make annuities and properly structured life insurance policies part of the sale. These strategies may allow you to not only reduce your taxes, but also increase your total untaxable income.

How Do Installment Sales Work?

Payments received from an installment sale consist of three parts.

Interest
- Gain/profit (taxed at the capital gains rate)
- Return of the seller's basis (cost) in the property (non-taxable).
- The interest must be reported as regular income. Taxes must be paid on it and the taxable portion of each distribution is received.

There are minimum interest requirements for installment sale interest, as it is considered regular income. The applicable federal rate (AFR), set each month by the IRS, is the minimum interest rate that must be charged. If you lend money at a rate lower than the AFR, you may owe tax on "imputed interest," as determined by the IRS.

Disadvantages of Installment Sales

There are also downsides to consider when using installment sales for real estate.

- For example, depreciation recapture requires you to pay a 25 percent tax on the excess amount of depreciation deductions taken beyond what is allowed under the straight-line method. This entire tax must be paid within the year you sell the property, even if you use an installment sale.
- Not everyone is eligible to use an installment sale.
- Sales of depreciable property to related parties are also prohibited unless it can be demonstrated that tax avoidance was not the main purpose of the sale. If the related party disposes of the property within two years, either through resale or another method, the remaining tax is due immediately.

Side note: The tax consequences of an installment sale may be different if the sale is conducted through the creation of a real estate note.

Chapter 5
Real Estate Tax Strategies

Real estate is a unique asset class. There are many ways to use real estate to build wealth and use it as a tax-savings tool.

Conceptually, individual real estate investors can pursue four different basic strategies:

- Buy and hold (using an LLC)
- Flipping, wholesaling (using an S Corp)
- Short-term rental property investing (Air BnB) - S Corps above $60,000
- Investing in notes, which you can do as a sole proprietor

Tip: Never hold assets inside an S Corp. Especially real estate. Why? There are several reasons:

- You don't get a step-up basis at death. When you keep real estate and other assets
- Inside an IRA, you lose the step-up basis benefit as well.
- When you want to refinance the property, it's considered a sale, and you'll be taxed on the profit.
- S-Corporations require you to pay a reasonable salary. What comes with a salary? Self-employment taxes. Yes, the S-Corp changes how your real estate is taxes and you will owe self-employment tax on all that income.

I know holding real estate and other assets inside a self-directed account is a common practice but think about the downfalls.

1. These are government-controlled accounts, and the government constantly changes the rules on these account.
2. There is nothing you can do about it because once your money or assets are inside this account, it's trapped.
3. You lose all tax benefits, such as depreciation. Your Real Estate does not get a step-up in basis.
4. Your money is trapped until retirement. You defer all taxes until retirement. You have no idea what the tax rates will be in retirement, and you have no idea how much of that money the government will let you keep.
5. You have Required Minimum Distributions, and your family will have to liquidate the account within ten years of your passing.

If you keep real estate inside a self-directed Roth account, you potentially eliminate the tax problem and RMD problem. I say potentially because they are still government-controlled accounts, and the rules can change.

Rental Real Estate Tax Strategy

Rental property isn't for everyone, but it does provide many benefits. Real estate can be a good way build wealth and can provide immense tax benefits. Tax write-offs can be incredible when you treat your rental property as a business.

The value of your property will grow tax-free until you sell, and several strategies allow you to avoid or delay paying the taxes.

- You can create tax-free cash flow.
- You can leverage your money to buy investment properties.
- You can enjoy financial growth that will outperform Wall Street.

Note: Your classification as a real estate investor is critical. The IRS may classify you as passive, active, or professional unless you take proactive steps to understand and elect the best classification for your situation. Here are some basics:

Passive investor. This means you take a "hands off" approach to real estate. You Hire a managing company to deal with all your real estate. This can be a good Way to grow wealth, but this is not a tax strategy. Your losses are deductible only against other passive income.

Active investor. To qualify, you simply need to make decisions concerning buying or selling property or hiring a property manager regarding your properties and check the proper box on your tax return. Losses are limited annually, however, to $25,000 and phase out completely at $150,000 of adjusted gross income for a married couple and $100,000 for an individual.

Real estate professional-As a real estate professional, a taxpayer is allowed to deduct 100 percent of their rental real estate losses against *any* other type of income. You must, however, meet a three-part test. If you are not considered a material participant, you will not be able to use losses from the activity to offset income from other sources, and the losses will be carried forward to future tax years.

How to Qualify for Real Estate Professional Status

To be considered a real estate professional for tax purposes, an individual or their spouse, must meet certain requirements set by the IRS. You must perform more than 750 hours of real estate services per property in real estate trades or businesses. Getting 750 hours of work per property is virtually impossible. However, a group election can be made to aggregate the 750 hours over all your properties.

1. The taxpayer must spend the majority of his or her time in real property businesses.
2. The taxpayer must spend 750 hours or more on qualifying real estate activities, with more time spent on this activity than any other. This means, if you have a full-time job, you will not qualify as a Real Estate Professional.
3. The taxpayer must *materially participate*

Real Property Trades and Activities

If you're involved in one or more of the activities listed below, the time spent performing your normal trade counts toward the hours required to meet real estate professional status. This makes REP status potentially much easier to achieve. However, you'll still have to materially participate in the rental activity itself.

Here are some activities that may contribute toward your material participation requirement.

- Real Property Development
- Redevelopment
- Construction
- Reconstruction
- Acquisition
- Property Management
- Conversion
- Rental
- Operation
- Brokerage (Real Estate only, not Mortgage)
- Leasing

Group Election

Group Elections offer a powerful tool for real estate professionals to consolidate material participation requirements. It allows consolidation of material participation across the entire group of properties rather than individually testing across multiple rental activities.

Qualifications for Group Election

To harness the benefits of Group Elections, Real Estate professionals must meet specific requirements.

Key Elements

The combined losses from the group can offset other active income, but any prior-year suspended losses remain suspended. If a property is sold within the group, associated losses are retained within the group and cannot offset gains from the sale.

A qualifying real estate professional seeking to combine all rental activities must formally elect to do so.

Simply consolidating all the taxpayer's rental activities into a single column on Schedule E, Supplemental Income and Loss, of Form 1040, U.S. Individual Income Tax Return, does not fulfill this obligation.

By submitting a statement along with the taxpayer's initial income tax return for the applicable tax year, a qualifying real estate professional exercises the choice to combine all rental real estate interests.

The tax return must include a statement of the taxpayer's qualification as a real estate professional for that tax year and their intention to make the election in accordance with Section 469(c)(7)(A).

You must list the specific addresses of the properties that will be grouped.

Revoking the Group Election

The ability to cancel the election is available to the taxpayer solely within the tax year where a significant shift in their facts and conditions takes place, or in a later year if the circumstances remain substantially different from those in the initial tax year of the election.

To reverse the election, the taxpayer is required to submit a statement alongside their original income tax return for the revocation year.

This document must include a statement confirming the taxpayer's intent to cancel the election under Section 469(c)(7)(Λ) and the circumstances that led to revoking the election.

Real Estate Dealer Status

Does the IRS classify you as a real estate business owner or an investor? The IRS has specific definitions for those terms, and your classification can affect the tax consequences of your real estate activities. The IRS could potentially view your real estate investment as a business rather than an investment. There are two main ways this could happen.

1. You are a real estate dealer.
2. You own rental properties that are classified as active rather than passive.

Consequences of Dealer Status

If you are engaged in a real estate business as a dealer or by providing *substantial services* to tenants (such as hotel-like services), you may face different tax consequences than if your real estate activities are considered investments.

If the IRS classifies you as a dealer rather than an investor, you will owe self-employment tax on your earnings. You'll also be barred from claiming depreciation deductions and will be subject to ordinary income tax rates on profits from sales. Additionally, you will not be able to use 1031 exchanges to defer tax on your sales.

An example of a Real Estate dealer is someone who "flips" properties. If you own some rental property and you flip some properties, be sure to keep separate business entities. Once your rental properties are in the same business entity as the properties you flip, they can be classified as inventory. When you sell these properties, they can be taxed as ordinary income instead of capital gains.

Short-Term Rental Properties

In general, short-term rentals are reported as passive rental activities on Schedule E of your tax return, and the income is not subject to self-employment tax. This can change if you provide substantial services to your guests.

Short-term rental rules are unique. There are four types of short-term rental properties:
1. "Business" short-term rentals *with* material participation
2. "Business" short-term rentals *without* material participation
3. Passive short-term rentals *with* material participation
4. Passive short-term rentals *without* material participation

All these classifications depend on the following three factors, and they will directly affect how your short-term rentals are taxed.

1. 1. Average stay of the tenant
2. 2. Were *substantial services* provided
3. 3. Did the taxpayer provide material participation?

Let's take a closer look at each of these three factors.

Factor 1: Average Rental Days a Tenant or Patron Stays at the Property

The first factor to consider is the average stay at your rental property.

Here, a key factor is whether the average stay is seven days or fewer. The seven-days-or-fewer rule applies, with the "average stay duration" taken over a year's time. Essentially, you divide your rental days by the number of renters.

If the average stay is *less* than seven days, you may report the operations on Schedule E (just like a typical long-term rental), and the income is *not* subject to self-employment tax (FICA). In this case, you also open the opportunity for ordinary loss treatment if you can show material participation (see below).

If the average stay is *more* than seven days, all is not lost. You must report the operations on Schedule E (just like a typical long-term rental). The income is *not* subject to self-employment tax (FICA). Note, however, that ordinary loss treatment is not available to you *even if* you can show material participation (see below).

Factor 2: Were Substantial Services Provided?

The next level of analysis comes down to the services you provide for tenants while they're staying at your property. We're talking here about what the IRS considers *substantial services.* There are pros and cons to providing substantial services, and they can affect your rental rates as well as the tax consequences.

Substantial Services and a "Business" Short-Term Rental

Substantial services can include services found in a hotel or bed and breakfast, such as:
- Providing meals
- Daily cleaning
- Maid service
- Travel arrangements
- Vehicles and other services commonly found in a hotel

If you provide substantial services to your guests, your short-term rental activity is no longer considered a passive rental activity. It's considered an active business, and it's reported on Schedule C. It is then subjected to a self-employment tax of 15.3 percent in addition to your ordinary income tax liability.

Factor 3: Did the Taxpayer Provide Material Participation?

Typically, to take flow-through passive rental losses as *ordinary losses,* one must qualify as a real estate professional. However, there is a unique loophole related to how short-term rentals are taxed.

If an owner can show personal *material participation,* then the rental losses on a short-term rental become ordinary losses.

To qualify as materially participating in the operations of your rental, a taxpayer must meet one of the following seven tests: *Not all seven,* but just one. Here are the tests, quoted directly from the IRS code.

What If I Have a Business Partner?

The 100-hour statistical significance test requires the partner to have spent at least 100 hours on the rental activity and no one else to have spent more time on it.

It may be difficult, however, for all partners in a multi-member LLC taxed as a partnership to meet these requirements. Each partner must then track their time and involvement in the rental activity to demonstrate that they have met the material participation tests and are eligible for tax benefits.

Are the Tax Benefits of Short-Term Rentals Available to All Business Partners?

For the tax benefits of short-term rentals to apply to all business partners, each partner must meet the requirements for material participation in the activity.

This includes engaging in the activity for more than 500 hours, having their involvement be statistically significant compared to the total engagement in the activity by all persons, spending at least 100 hours on the activity and no one else spending more time, and being able to track and substantiate their time and the time of others.

It can be difficult for one individual to meet these requirements, and it can be even more challenging for a group of partners working together. Additionally, in a multi-member LLC taxed as a partnership, it may be difficult to identify enough activities for each partner to meet the substantial involvement standards required to classify their share of losses as non-passive.

Cost Segregation

Cost segregation is a tax strategy that allows a business or individual to save on taxes by identifying and separating various components of a real estate property. The IRS allows the owner to depreciate the cost of a property over a period of time intended to approximate its useful life. A property is made up of many different components, however, and each has its own useful life and depreciation rate.

A cost segregation study can identify and separate these components into personal property, real property, or land improvements, which can be depreciated over shorter periods. In general, 20 to 30 percent of a property's purchase price can be reclassified under shorter-class lives.

Separating these components can:

- Allow you to take advantage of shorter depreciation periods and accelerated deductions.
- It can also make it easier to write off the remaining undepreciated assets when they are replaced, thus saving money on taxes.
- Additionally, reclassifying assets from real estate to personal property can lower the value subject to real estate taxes and shift income to long-term capital gain.

Cost segregation makes the most sense for landlords who are considered real estate professionals for tax purposes or expect to be eligible for the passive loss limits.

Here are some examples of components for which cost segregation is permitted.

Real Property
- Steel structure
- Roof
- Walls/doors (not load-bearing walls)
- HVAC systems

Personal Property
- Carpets
- Cabinets/countertops
- Blinds
- Specialty plumbing/lighting

Land Improvements
- Parking lots
- Irrigation systems
- Retaining walls
- Landscaping, trees, and shrubs

If a property can be removed without damaging the building structure, it may be classified as personal property.

A general rule is that if an asset and equipment or machinery are closely related and would be retired at the same time, they may qualify as personal property. For example, TVs with a depreciation period of five years and associated electrical outlets may also depreciate over five years. Moreover, appliances in an apartment complex with specific outlets, such as a washing machine or dryer, may also qualify as personal property.

Be cognitive that cost segregation can lead you to have more depreciation recapture when selling the property. This isn't a problem if you prepare for it. Afterall, the Time Value of Money, and saving taxes up front is a good thing. But I have seen investors not plan for the depreciation recapture and owe $100's of thousands of dollars in taxes. Oil and gas may be a strategy to avoid this mess.

1031 and 712 Exchanges

Most people who've been involved in real estate are at least passingly familiar with the 1035 tax-free exchange of like-kind properties.

The 1031 exchange makes it possible to sell your old rental property and buy a new one while deferring capital gains taxes—potentially indefinitely. That's a great deal for those who still want to be landlords, with all the hassles that potentially entail.

Most real estate investors love 1031 Exchanges and do constantly. The problem is you're kicking the tax can down the road. Sure, you can do it indefinitely until you die. Perhaps your kids will get a step-up in basis? Perhaps the tax law will change, and Congress will do a way with step-up basis. Or what if you need capital at some point and you need to sell the property? A couple alternative strategies to a 1031 can be a 712 Exchange, oil & gas, or buy another property and have a cost-segregation study performed.

But what if you no longer want to be a landlord?

Well, that's where the much less well-known Section 721 exchange comes in. With a Section 721 exchange, you can ditch the hassles of traditional property ownership and management and unload direct responsibility for your rental property while still avoiding huge capital gains from the sale of your property.

Here's how it works: Instead of selling your property outright for cash or exchanging it for another rental property that you'd have to play landlord on, *you can use Section 721 to trade your property for shares in the investment trust that buys the property from you.*

Your shares can earn you a steady income and, with time, will hopefully increase in value. Meanwhile, this deal structure allows you to transition from being an *active* investor to a *passive* one. You receive dividend income from the investment company in retirement, providing financial security.

A 721 exchange also gets you shares in a diversified portfolio. Instead of owning a single piece of real estate, you now own interest in a portfolio of various property types and locations; this helps protect your investment from unpredictable market changes and individual property risk.

1031 *vs.* 721 Exchanges

Here are several key differences between Section 1031 and Section 721 exchanges:

Ownership. When you trade your property on a 721 exchange, you don't own that real estate anymore; you only own shares. You no longer have control over the property. When you trade your property on a 1031 exchange property, you're still the owner and in control of all the decision making.

Responsibility. With ownership comes responsibility. If you can't find tenants for your property, you'll pay for the vacancy costs. The costs of maintenance also come out of your wallet. When you transfer your property with a 721 exchange, you no longer need to worry about the burdens of maintenance and management like you do if you use a 1031 exchange and remain the active owner.

Liquidity. Shares in a trust may be more liquid than a piece of property.

Diversification. A 721 exchange potentially facilitates instant diversification by giving you immediate fractional ownership of an extensive portfolio of various property types and locations, rather than one single property.

Income. Owning an investment property can net you regular rental income, but so can distributions from your portfolio shares. Either way, you'll likely earn monthly or quarterly income from your investment. With a 721 exchange, however, you'll begin earning passive income. Rain or shine, work or vacation, you'll receive distributions. The same isn't true when you are responsible for property investments.

Note: Not every property qualifies for a 721 exchange. When 721 isn't an option, the owner can take advantage of 1031 equity into a Delaware Statutory Trust, which does qualify as an "asset in kind."

Chapter 6
Are You Grossing $1 million a Year, or More?

COVID-19 taught us many lessons. One of the most important lessons it taught us is, we need to be prepared for anything, including government mandated shutdowns. During Covid, the government shut down an estimated 1.6 million establishments, according to the U.S. Bureau of Labor Statistics.

As the government shut down businesses, most of the businesses discovered they did not have business interruption coverage and many businesses went bankrupt. As business interruption claims were denied by insurance carriers throughout COVID-19, and it became apparent that most businesses need alternative solutions to protect assets, mitigate risks, and ensure financial security in today's changing world.

In today's global business environment, there are an infinite number of risks facing businesses, including government shutdowns, cyber threats, supply change disruptions, and even bank collapse. Unfortunately, traditional commercial insurance does not always provide the coverage business owners need to protect their business or their family from these risks. Unavailable coverage or coverage that is too expensive, can leave business owners exposed to significant risks within their business.

There is a solution for many businesses. It's an 831 (b) plan, otherwise referred to as a Captive Insurance Company. These plans were first introduced in 1986 under section 831(b) of the Internal Revenue Code. These plans allow businesses to set aside tax-deferred funds through the formation of a Captive Insurance program.

It's important to note, this is not a tax strategy. It's a risk-mitigation strategy that just happens to help you shelter large amounts of money from taxation.

How captive insurance works:

Step 1: Identify a specific insurable business or investment risk. Here are some common examples of risks that businesses use captive insurance companies to offset:

- Property Risks. Damage or loss of property due to natural disasters, fire, or vandalism.
- Liability Risks. Legal liabilities from product defects, professional services, or general liability claims.
- Workers' Compensation. Costs associated with employee injuries or occupational illnesses.

- Business Interruption. Loss of income due to disruptions like supply chain issues or natural disasters.
- Cyber Risks. Data breaches, cyber-attacks, and related security incidents.
- Employee Benefits. Health, dental, and disability insurance for employees.
- Directors and Officers Liability. Personal liabilities of company directors and officers arising from their decisions.
- Reputational Risk. Losses associated with public relations issues and brand damage.
- Supply Chain Risks. Delays or disruptions in the supply chain that impact production and delivery.
- Environmental Risks. Pollution, hazardous waste management, and other regulatory liabilities.
- Political Risks. Losses from expropriation, political instability, or regulatory changes.
- Product Recall. Costs and liabilities related to recalling defective products.

Businesses pay third-party insurance companies to offload these types of risks all the time. The problem with the traditional insurance model is that the traditional model can be expensive and not suit the needs of the business. Not only that, once the business owner pays for those expenses, the money is gone forever. Captive insurance companies can be a more efficient and tax-advantaged way for you to take those premiums you're paying to some other company and keep them in house.

Step 2: Establish a Captive Insurance Company

Like any insurance company, these companies are subject to real capitalization and financial stability rules. They are licensed to issue real insurance contracts with real underwriting and real risk sharing.

Step 3: Your operating business will buy insurance from your Captive Insurance Company

You'll pay premiums to the captive and deduct them just like any other insurance expense you currently pay. Those premiums are held in a reserve account. Funds that accumulate this reserve account can be used for investments or can be used for other business purposes. A captive insurance company allows a business owner to retain those premium dollars for your own business, rather than somebody else's. When contractual liabilities arise, you can file a claim against the 831(b) Plan like a traditional insurance policy.

Tax Treatment

Infernal Revenue Code (I.R.C.) Section 831(b) is a U.S. tax law that provides specific tax benefits to certain insurance companies. The captive insurance company must qualify as an insurance company for tax purposes under these rules.

The 831(b) election allows specific insurance companies to receive up to $2.8 million, in premiums, in 2024, without paying any income taxes on those premiums. The exemption amount changes every year. This allows your company to get a tax deduction for its insurance costs, as it currently does, and allows

YOUR Captive Insurance Company to receive that money, tax free. The Captive Insurance Company elects to hold these reserves in a C-Corp. The reserves can then be invested.

- Under Section 831(b), there is a 0% Federal income tax on the captive's underwriting profits, up to the exemption amount.
- It pays income tax only on its investment income.
- The investment income and realized gains, generated by plan reserves, are taxable at the
- C-Corp rate, not ordinary income tax rate.
- Plan participants, or shareholders may elect to distribute reserves by declaring a dividend. Dividend distributions taken by shareholders are taxable to the individual at the qualified dividend rate. This rate can be 0%.

Basically, the money put into the 831 (b) plan would typically be an expense and the business would never see this money again. Once it enters the 831 (b) plan, you, as the business owner, retain control over these funds. When integrated with estate plans, the wealth protection and accumulation benefits can be substantial.

A list of Benefits

- Customized insurance policies that address their specific risks.
- Cover the risks not addressed by traditional insurers.
- Assets in your captive insurance company are segregated from your primary business assets.
- Allows a business owner to defer income to address tomorrow's risks.
- tax-deferred reserves allow business owners to weather the storm when catastrophe strikes.
- Improve cash flow predictability and balances
- Minimize taxes
- Increase asset portfolio liquidity and avoid the volatility of the cyclical insurance market
- Reduce insurance costs
- Expand wealth accumulation options
- Protect assets
- Reduce asset transfer costs
- Stabilize insurance costs
- Reinsurance access
- Generate additional income through investment activity.

Compliance

Designed and operated correctly, Captive Insurance Companies provide substantial wealth creation and protection. However, if the 831(b) election is abused, the IRS can deny the deduction to the operating company who paid the premiums, and tax the captive on its premium income.

The captive insurance company must be operating in good faith as an insurance company. This means the captive is set up and managed for genuine risk management purposes, not to achieve tax benefits.

The captive insurance company must comply with the insurance regulations in its jurisdiction of domicile, as 831(b) plans are subject to U.S. state regulations, including capital and solvency requirements, corporate governance standards, and financial reporting obligations.

A Few Examples of Who May Be a Good Fit

- A property management company
- Successful businesses with gross revenue over $1 million per year
- high net worth families
- General contractors, agencies, and other businesses using subcontractors
- Real Estate Investor
- Manufactures
- Medical Professionals
- General Contractors

Key Disclaimer:
Tax incentives are obviously important. HOWEVER, non-tax reasons must drive all captive formation decisions.

Chapter 7
Taxes in Retirement

Would you like to cut ties with the IRS in retirement?

The single biggest factor that causes retirees to overpay taxes in retirement is contributing the bulk of their retirement to a 401(k), IRA, or other qualified accounts.

I know. I know. You've been told your entire life to defer taxes until retirement because you'll be in a lower tax bracket in retirement. For most folks, this simply isn't true. It's a financial myth that tricks people into locking up their money in these accounts. Then Wall Street uses your money in these accounts to grow their wealth. At the end of the day, you've let Wall Street use your money for most of your life, and you are left with pennies.

The only way you end up in a lower tax bracket in retirement is if you retire poor or INTENTIONALLY create a tax-free retirement.

Let's look at some facts. As of June 13, 2024, the current US national debt is nearly $35,000,000,000 (that's $35 trillion) and rapidly growing. Represented per citizen, that is nearly $105,000 each. As not all citizens pay taxes, the US national debt represents nearly $270,000 per US taxpayer. (Source http://www. usdebt-clock.org/)

The interest on the debt is nearly $868 billion. The social security unfunded liability is nearly $15 trillion, and the Medicare unfunded liability is nearly $80 trillion. The prescription drug unfunded liability is nearly $20 trillion, and the healthcare unfunded liability is over $9 trillion.

The federal deficit was nearly $1.7 trillion in 2023 and is expected to be $2 trillion a year from 2024 to 2044, based on the CBO (Congressional Budget Office) projections. Where do you think taxes and inflation are going? They must go up.

If your 401(k) or IRA grows, so does the government's share of your account, since the government (both state and federal) is your business partner in retirement. These accounts are taxed at the income tax level, which makes them the lowest-hanging fruit for tax increases.

The question is, are you prepared for your retirement account to be a sitting duck for tax increases and for the government to have a permanent tax lien against your retirement account? Are you prepared to have half of your retirement, or more, taken by the government? Unfortunately, most people are not. Taking such a massive tax hit will make the difference between a comfortable retirement and struggling to make ends meet for basic living expenses.

If you don't have a plan for your money, don't worry. The government has a plan for your money. They will use it to fund whatever pork programs they deem necessary or send it off to other countries.

This kind of hit to your financial future doesn't have to happen. You don't have to contribute to these accounts. You can create a plan to move your tax-deferred funds from accounts that will be taxed forever into accounts that will never be taxed!

Sure, you can do a back door conversion into a Roth, but you still have the problem of a huge backdoor Roth transfer, which means a huge spike in your taxes! If you use this account to pay for taxes, you'll lose a significant amount of its value. Don't you want to keep as much money as possible in this tax-free vehicle? You better have the funds available elsewhere to pay the tax bill. And, in case you haven't heard, the Roth conversation may soon be taken away by Congress.

Do you want the government as your business partner in retirement, or would you like to kick the government out of your retirement plan? If you do not trust the government, the best course of action is to kick them out of your retirement plan as quickly as possible. If you plan for them correctly, taxes are one of the most manageable risks to control in retirement.

Four financial vehicles give you tax-free retirement income: HSA, Roth IRA, Roth 401(k), and life insurance. Doesn't it make sense to take the tax risk off the table and generate as much tax-free income in retirement as you possibly can?

HSAs

With the increase in medical costs, why would you not want one of these accounts?

Roth IRAs

Traditional IRAs and qualified plan contributions let you deduct your money going in, which may feel great now. However, when you withdraw your money, you will face a minor issue: TAXES. If you want to take the tax risk off the table for your retirement, a Roth IRA may be a good option. However, there are other ways to create nontaxable income in retirement.

Roth IRA Disadvantages

- Low annual contribution limits: It's impossible to put enough money into a Roth for your retirement. For 2024, the maximum amount of money you can put into a Roth IRA is $7,000 if you're under the age of fifty and $8,000 if you're over the age of fifty.
- You may make too much money to contribute to a Roth. If you're single and your modified adjusted gross income (MAGI) exceeds $146,000, you can only make a partial contribution. Once your MAGI reaches $153,000, you are no longer eligible to contribute. If you're married and filing jointly, your phase-out starts at $218,000. Once your MAGI reaches $228,000, you are no longer eligible to contribute.
- A Roth IRA does not alleviate your current tax problem; it simply changes the timing of your tax problem.
- A Roth IRA, however, does not help eliminate other retirement risks, such as market losses, long-term care risks, cash flow risks, asset diversification risks, sequence of return risks, or liquidity risks. And don't forget, your money is trapped in that account until you retire.
- There will be a 10 percent penalty on withdrawals before age fifty-nine and a half unless the withdrawal falls within one of the exceptions to that usual rule.

Life Insurance

When you hear the term "life insurance," what do you think about? You should think about asset protection, tax-free wealth, tax-free generational wealth, and your *Family Banking System*.

Most people think about the death benefit, but life insurance has many benefits that no other asset class provides. It can be used to protect your assets and create your Family Banking System. Life insurance can be used to provide tax-free passive cash flow in retirement and protect you against the costs of long-term care. It is also a protected asset. In many states, it's fully, or partially protected from lawsuits and divorce.

There's a belief out there that the wealthy don't need life insurance. But the wealthiest and most powerful families on the planet put money into life insurance. Life insurance is the reason these families have remained wealthy and powerful. A simple strategy to continue grow and continue generational wealth is for every member of the family to get a life insurance policy on them when they are born. They use this as a *Family Banking System* throughout their life. When they pass away, the death benefit goes to the Family Trust.

Banks put $100s billions of dollars into life insurance. Corporations put hundreds of billions of dollars into life insurance. Why is that? What do they know that you don't? Well, they know a lot.

The Design/Structure of Your Policy Matters

Permanent life insurance has two main components: a death benefit and a cash value. A policy can be designed to provide a high death benefit, or it can be designed to provide a high cash value.

If a policy is designed to provide a high death benefit, then most of your premium goes toward the cost of insurance to create a high death benefit, and the policy's cash value will grow slowly. Policies designed for a big death benefit are not favorable for retirement income or for the *Family Banking Strategy*, but they are favorable for generational wealth.

The death benefit is much smaller if a policy is designed to provide high cash value. Most of the money you put into the policy goes toward the cash value, and the cash value will grow more quickly. When we design a policy focusing on cash accumulation, we pump as much money into it as possible while maintaining its function as life insurance. Policies that are designed for high cash accumulation are ideal for retirement planning and *Family Banking Systems*.

Banks and corporations use permanent life insurance policies to provide retirement income for their executives. Along the way, they hold liquid capital in these accounts. Why are banks and Wall Street using this strategy but telling you not to? It's because they know something you don't.

At the end of this book, I included a chapter on the many ways corporations and business owners use life insurance to increase their wealth and increase asset protection.

Chapter 8

Life Insurance as Your *Family Banking System*

The common mantra I hear is, "Buy term and invest the difference." But life insurance has nothing to do with investing. When utilizing a High Cash-Value, Dividend-Paying Life Insurance Policy, it gives you the ability to control the banking function in your life.

Walt Disney used the money inside his policy to start his empire when no bank would give him a loan. Ray Krok used his policies to grow a small business named McDonald's. When all else was failing during the Great Depression, JC Penny used his life insurance policies to keep from going bankrupt.

This strategy has been used by professional athletes, coaches, rappers, and the affluent.

There are many names for this strategy: *Bank on Yourself, Become Your Own Banker,* and *Infinite Banking.* I refer to the strategy as a *Family Banking System.*

Quick history.

The *Infinite Banking* concept, as we understand it today, was brought to light by R. Nelson Nash in the 1980s. He did not discover or create how life insurance is used, but he learned how to maximize the benefits. The 1980s was a period of very high interest rates, and it put tremendous pressure on him through his highly leveraged real estate investments.

Nelson realized he could access money through his various life insurance policies at only 5 to 8 percent, while the bankers were charging him up to 23 percent. He used policy loans to start paying off the bankers.

Once the debt was transferred to life insurance companies, Nash was able to repay the money on his schedule and with a much better interest rate. Because his money stayed in the policy and continued to grow, the growth in the life insurance cash values offset the interest he paid on those short-term loans, so there was no net cost over time.

What started as a quick way to transfer debt from interest-hungry bankers to more reasonable rates grew into the very popular concept of using whole life insurance values as a reserve from which to finance all types of purchases without borrowing from banks.

Nash started teaching the idea, wrote the book *Becoming Your Own Banker* in 1999, and traveled around the country teaching seminars for life insurance agents and financial advisors during the early twenty-first century.

Is *Infinite Banking* a Scam?

Life insurance is not a scam. Dollar for dollar, there is no other financial tool that can build generational wealth better than life insurance. Life insurance is a financial vehicle used for many strategies. A few of the strategies include:

- Retirement plans for business owners and individuals
- "Golden handcuffs" and incentives for employees
- Business succession/exit planning,
- Estate planning
- Building generational wealth.

Misinformation

There is a lot of misinformation and misunderstanding surrounding *Infinite Banking* and life insurance. People often confuse the term *Infinite Banking* with life insurance. Generally, when people think about life insurance, they are completely focused on the death benefit. The death benefit is not the primary focus when implementing this strategy. The primary when implementing this strategy is to maximize the cash value of a policy on day one.

This is an important distinction and a big reason many people do not understand it. Those who are against it simply do not understand how it works. The biggest argument against life insurance is that the person against it almost always compares the low guaranteed returns of whole life to the returns of a Roth IRA.

This argument fails for several reasons

It fails to address the actual concept of "*Infinite Banking*." The concepts of *Infinite Banking* and investing in the stock market serve different purposes. When the financial industry talks about returns, they talk about the AVERAGE rate of returns. They do not look at the TOTAL returns. *Infinite Banking* is centered around total returns and leveraging your money to create more cash flow, which leads to more wealth. It involves creating a pile of money that never stops growing and isn't subjected to stock market losses.

It allows you to create a system that mimics a bank and allows you to recapture the money you're currently giving to the banks and credit cards. What other financial vehicle allows you to recapture all your lost interest while building wealth AND allows you to invest your money elsewhere? NONE! And do not forget the death benefit.

Average returns from the stock market refer to watching the paper value of a portfolio go up and down, side to side, and where it ends up, is anyone's guess. At the end of this book, you'll find a chapter on, "Why the Average Returns of Your Portfolio Do Not Matter".

Infinite Banking is a financial strategy, and life insurance is the financial vehicle we prefer to use for the strategy. Of course, some people have scammed themselves by not using the strategy correctly, not paying their premiums, or not paying their loans back. They find it easier to blame the concept on someone else.

People have certainly been "scammed" or ripped off by not understanding the process or by working with an "advisor" that does not understand the process. This typically happens by buying a life insurance policy designed for a large death benefit or by buying an indexed universal life policy as an *Infinite Banking* policy.

I mentioned there are many financial vehicles that can be used to build *a Family Banking System*, so let's look at some of these financial vehicles to see why we prefer life insurance as the financial vehicle.

Your Margin Account Banking System

A common strategy used by billionaires to generate tax-free cash flow is to leverage their stocks. They put their stocks up as collateral and borrow money from the bank or a broker. The interest they pay on this borrowed money is tax-free. They pay interest on this borrowed money, but the interest is much cheaper than the taxes they would pay.

A margin account allows you to borrow funds from a broker to buy securities using your existing investments as collateral. This allows your stock to continue growing in value (or losing value).

While margin accounts can provide leverage and potentially amplify investment gains, they can also amplify investment losses. Is it worth the risk?

1. Risk of Losses

    Margin trading involves borrowing money to invest. Suppose the value of your investment in the margin account declines. If that happens, you are likely to face margin calls, which require you to deposit additional funds, or you may be forced to sell securities to meet the margin requirement. If you cannot meet the margin calls, the brokerage firm may sell the securities in the margin account to cover the losses, potentially resulting in significant losses and the erosion of the family's wealth.

2.   Volatility and Market Risk

The stock market can be volatile, and the value of investments in a margin account can fluctuate widely. This can result in substantial losses.

3.   Limited Access to Funds

Margin accounts may restrict the way the money is used. The amount that can be borrowed is typically limited by the value of the securities used as collateral. This can limit the family's flexibility and access to funds for other financial needs outside of the investments held in the margin accounts.

4.   Complexity and Risk of Margin Trading

Margin trading involves complex rules and regulations. You must understand the risks, requirements, and potential consequences before using a margin account as a family banking system. It requires careful monitoring of investment positions, margin levels, and market conditions to manage the risks effectively. If you want to just set-it and forget it

You can use a 401(k)

When you put your money into a 401(k), IRA, or other qualified accounts, your money is locked up and in a financial vehicle the government controls. The accounts are nothing more than sections of the tax code. The government can change the rules on these accounts at any time, including how much they take in taxes.

1.   Your 401(k) is a government-controlled financial vehicle.
2.   Your 401(k) is a tax trap.
3.   You're limited to what you can borrow money for.
4.   Your 401(k) plan dictates your repayment schedule.
5.   Your 401(k) offers no guarantees.
6.   Your 401(k) offers no safety.
7.   There are early withdrawal penalties.
8.   There are limitations on how much you can borrow.

Let's see what borrowing from your 401(k) looks like.

Most 401(k)s allow you to borrow up to 50 percent of the funds vested in the account or $50,000, whichever is less, for up to five years.

1.   Repayment will cost you more than your original contributions.

An alleged benefit of a 401(k) loan is that you're simply borrowing from yourself with little to no costs. This allegation quickly becomes questionable once you examine how you'll have to repay the money.

Keep in mind that the funds you're borrowing were contributed to the 401(k) on a pre-tax basis. But you'll be paying back the loan with *after-tax* money.

Let's pretend your effective tax rate is 15 percent. Every $1 you earn to repay your loan leaves you with only 85 cents to repay that loan. The rest goes to income tax. Don't forget about all the other taxes as well. In other words, making your fund whole again essentially requires about six to eight times more work.

2. The low interest rate overlooks opportunity costs.

    While you're borrowing funds from your account, they won't be earning a return. Those missed earnings need to be balanced against the supposed break you're getting for lending yourself money at a low interest rate.

    It is common to assume that a 401(k) loan is effectively cost-free since the interest is paid back into the participant's own 401(k) account. There is an "opportunity" cost equal to the amount of growth you've lost on the borrowed funds.

    If a 401(k) account has a total return of 8 percent for a year of borrowed money from it, the cost of that loan is effectively 8 percent. But then you must compound that last growth every year until the day your heirs deplete that account after you pass on. That could be fifty, sixty years, or more of lost wealth.

3. You may contribute less to the fund while you have the loan.

    If you borrow money from your 401(k) account, some plans have a provision that prohibits you from making additional contributions until the loan balance is repaid. Even if your plan doesn't stipulate this, you may be unable to afford to make contributions while you're repaying the loan.

4. If your financial situation deteriorates, you could lose even more money.

    So far, we've been assuming you'll be able to make the scheduled payments back to your account on time. But what if you default on a 401(k) loan? The loan is converted to a withdrawal, and the outstanding loan balance will be subject, at minimum, to taxation at your current income tax rate. If you're under the age of fifty-five and a half, you'll also be assessed a 10% early-withdrawal penalty on the amount you've borrowed.

5. A Job Loss or Departure

    Plan sponsors may require an employee to repay the full outstanding balance of a loan if he or she terminates employment or if the plan is terminated. If the employee is unable to repay the loan, then the employer will treat it as a distribution.

When you consider all this, a 401(k) doesn't seem like it's a good financial vehicle to hold your capital in.

Your Shoebox Banking System

You may laugh at this, but remember, banking is a process. You can even use a shoebox because the family banking system is a process. However, there are some drawbacks to using a shoebox. Unfortunately, a shoebox is not a secure place to store money, and there is no interest or growth potential.

Your HELOC Banking System

Real estate is often used as a banking system of sorts. A HELOC is a revolving line of credit secured by your home's equity, allowing you to borrow against the value of your home. Similar to a credit card, you can borrow up to a certain limit, repay the borrowed amount, and borrow again as needed during the draw period.

Building enough equity to function in this manner can take a long time, and the costs can be high. When you get a loan, you may have fees, closing costs, and appraisal costs. The lending institution may also restrict you. You may not qualify for a loan. And as interest rates increase, your borrowing costs can dramatically increase.

Why Whole Life (WL) Insurance?

Life insurance has characteristics no other financial vehicle has. It offers uninterrupted compound interest, tax-free access to money, safety, guaranteed growth, and liquidity, which allows you to create a system that operates more like a banking system than an insurance policy. Even though it's technically a loan, it acts more like a line of credit. As soon as you pay back a portion of the loan, you have access to that capital.

No matter what the stock market or the economy is doing, it allows you to create an additional stream of passive income that will enhance the overall growth of your other investments. It does this through contractual guarantees. The companies we use have been doing this for upward of 160–180 years.

Most assets are "either/or." You can either buy a rental house *or* put money into the stock market. You can pay off debt *or* save money. Life insurance is an "and/both" asset. It allows you to do multiple things at the same time by leveraging the money inside your policy.

Not only will you have access to every dollar you put into your policies at some point, but you will also have access to tax-free cash flow, protection from creditors, and a death benefit above the cash value on day one. This becomes a self-completing savings strategy. Should anything happen to you, your policy will still pay to take care of your kids or supplement an income for your spouse.

A Safe Place to Store Capital

Part of becoming wealthy involves getting lucky. Luck is where preparation meets opportunity. Opportunity has a way of finding those prepared when you have liquidity, you'll have an opportunity to frow your wealth when the opportunity arises. Maintaining sufficient liquidity and access to capital is key to taking control and capitalizing on opportunities when they arise. Liquidity gives you flexibility and safety. When the sky starts falling and cash is truly king the most profitable opportunities during your lifetime will present themselves to you

Banks are great for transactions, but a terrible place to hold your liquid capita. Life insurance is a great place to store your liquid capital.

Your liquid capital must reside somewhere. For centuries, most people have held their money inside banks. These banks are already taking your deposits and depositing them into life insurance policies for THEIR benefit. Why don't you cut out the middleman? You can store your capital in properly structured permanent life insurance policies. It is the perfect warehouse to store your working capital, so you can deploy it when opportunities present themselves.

Every dollar you put into someone else's bank helps them create wealth. Once you put money into someone else's system, what happens to your money from there? You can save it, invest in it, spend it, or give it away.

Once that money leaves your coffers, you lose all the future value of your money. Another institution captures the future value of your money. It's True, your money can buy assets, which can create cash flow or create a return and increase your wealth, but the dollars themselves no longer provide value.

The *Family Banking System* allows you to buy these same assets AND maintain the future value of every dollar that crosses your balance sheet. So, even though you are using your money, your money continues to grow in value for future use.

I'm not advocating for you to just leave your money sit somewhere and do nothing for you. That's not how you create wealth. You create wealth with your money by putting it to work.

One of the contractual guarantees of life insurance is that you have access to the cash inside your policy. Contrary to popular belief, you don't borrow your own money, or borrow "from your policy." You actually borrow money from the life insurance company's general account. I would like to say it's a similar process to how you borrow money from a bank, but the process is much more simple.

Most investment opportunities—even great ones—put your money to work in only one place. You put your money in, earn a return, and take your money out. For instance, when you put money into the stock market, it only grows, or loses, in the stock market. When you buy real estate, it only grows in real estate.

Life insurance is called an "and" asset because it offers the unparalleled opportunity to put your money to work in multiple places at the same time. When you include a properly structured permanent life insurance policy in your financial plan, you can borrow AGAINST your policy and use the money to invest in real estate, buy businesses, or invest it in your own business.

You can even borrow against your policy to invest in the stock market. This means your money grows in two places at the same time. Not only does it grow in two places at the same time, but you have financial protection from death, divorce, sickness, market losses, and long-term care.

Yes, you do pay interest to the life insurance company. The interest is simple interest. The money inside your policy continues to compound. The rate of growth in your policy will outpace the loan rate.

These costs can be offset by the credits that your policy continues to receive (even while your equity is out on loan doing double duty for you). As a policy owner, you benefit from that. As a policy owner of a mutual life insurance company, you are a part owner and receive a dividend.

Unlike bank loans or credit cards, you control when you pay back the loans. There are no payment schedules or minimum payment amounts. Each time you make a payment against your loan, you end up at a higher spot on your compound curve because your money was never withdrawn, and it continued to grow.

Chapter 9
How Does Your Family Banking System Create Certainty in Retirement?

"We are heading to a future where we'll have to double federal taxes or cut federal spending by 60%!"
—DAVID WALKER, U.S. FORMER COMPTROLLER GENERAL

There is a common mantra echoed throughout the financial community: "You won't *need* whole life insurance in retirement." This is because they do not understand how life insurance works. The most common argument against life insurance is about the "low" returns, so I added a section after this named "Why the Average Returns of Your Portfolio Do Not Matter" to help you understand why this "advice" is misleading and detrimental to your retirement. What's more important than the average rate of return is:

- the timing of your losses
- the magnitude of your losses
- the fees you pay
- the taxes you pay
- the lost opportunity costs.

There are many different types of permanent life insurance and an infinite number of ways to design policies, so it's crucial to work with someone who understands life insurance. When you design your policy for retirement purposes, it protects you from many retirement risks, such as:

- Inflation risk
- Market risk and sequence of return risks
- Tax Increase
- Long-term care
- Cash flow
- Longevity risk, which is the biggest risk because it amplifies all the other risks.

<u>Risk Buffer in Retirement</u>

Whole-life insurance is completely uncorrelated to the stock market. It is contractually guaranteed to increase in value every year. Whole-life insurance gives you a solid foundation on which you can build a holistic financial plan. If there is a market crash and a portion of your assets are allocated to whole life insurance during retirement, you could take your immediate income needs from your policy and allow your stocks to recover.

<u>Life Insurance Is a Tax Buffer</u>

With taxes likely to increase, do you want to have as much tax-free cash flow as possible, or do you want to continue risking all your retirement income to tax risks? Roth IRAs are a good source for tax-free income, but they still come with market risks, and they trap your money throughout your lifetime.

> Life insurance gives you an opportunity to "time your tax" by controlling the amount of taxable retirement distributions you take each year.

So, you have a Roth 401(k)? Great! You still have no access to your capital. You have no control over what you invest in. You're stuck with mutual funds, target-date funds, and a few other options designed to steal your wealth through fees and market losses.

Fees in these accounts typically range between 1 and 2 percent a year. Over thirty years, you're losing 30–60 percent of the money you put into your account, and the growth of your account, to fees. Everything has fees, but you must look at the value you get for the fees. Leaving your money trapped in an account that you have no control over is not beneficial.

Perhaps you don't *need* any whole life insurance during retirement, but you will probably *want* it for its tax treatment and its guaranteed income. Most of your other sources of retirement income will be taxable in some way, shape, or form. None of the following are immune from Uncle Sam:

- Rental real estate
- Taxable brokerage accounts
- Tax-deferred annuities
- Social security
- Deferred compensation plans
- Retirement accounts: IRAs, 401(k)s, profit-sharing plans, defined-benefit pensions, etc.

Life Insurance Provides Guaranteed Income and Adds Security to Your Retirement

Policy withdrawals or loans can be used to supplement your retirement income.

You will have guaranteed expenses in retirement. Shouldn't you have a guaranteed income? Guaranteed income can help cover essential expenses, such as housing, food, and healthcare, ensuring that you can maintain a certain standard of living even if other sources of income fluctuate.

Guaranteed income allows you to be more secure and flexible in adjusting your retirement plan. It helps you weather unexpected expenses or changes in your financial situation.

Death Benefit in Retirement

Death is the only guarantee you have in life. If you knew that your spouse and children would receive tax-free money at your death, wouldn't you worry less about spending down your assets? Of course, you would. That death benefit allows you to more aggressively spend down other assets in your portfolio while you and your spouse are healthy and can enjoy that money together. The death benefit is especially important for women because they typically live longer than men.

A life insurance policy's death benefit is a source of tax-free cash for final expenses and estate settlement costs, including estate and inheritance taxes. Life insurance will help create and protect your legacy.

YOU CAN LEAVE MORE MONEY TO YOUR FAVORITE ORGANIZATION

Do you enjoy giving money to the church? Or do you have a charity you want to leave money to when you're no longer here? You can buy a life insurance policy and name your favorite organization as the beneficiary.

You can donate money every year to your favorite organization. But no matter how much you contribute, you will never be able to leave as much money to the organization as you could if you bought a life insurance policy and named them the beneficiary.

Not only that, depending on how you structure the policy, you have access to the cash value throughout your lifetime. Or, you can structure the policy in a way that makes it tax deductible.

Chronic Illness Rider or Accelerated Death Benefit

A feature included in some life insurance policies allows you to receive a tax-free advance on your life insurance death benefit while alive. Sometimes you must pay an extra premium to add this feature to your life insurance policy. Sometimes the insurance company includes it in the policy for little or no cost.

Depending on your policy, you may be able to receive a cash advance on your life insurance policy's death benefit if:

This feature can be used if any of the following illnesses or conditions are diagnosed:

- Invasive Life-Threatening Cancer Major Burns
- Stroke
- Coma
- Major Heart Attack
- Aplastic Anemia
- End-stage Renal Failure
- Benign Brain Tumor
- Major Organ Transplant
- Aortic Aneurysm
- ALS (Amyotrophic Lateral Sclerosis)
- Heart Valve Replacement
- Blindness due to Diabetes Coronary
- Artery Bypass Graft Surgery
- Paralysis of two or more Limbs
- Kidney disease
- Or are terminally ill

Health issues continue to increase as our food and air are pumped with toxins. The risk of health problems also increases as we get older. If you experience these problems, how will you continue working? How will you pay your bills? How will you contribute to your retirement? Life insurance may be a viable option.

If these problems occur after retirement, how will you pay the bills? Will you sell off assets, pay taxes, and then pay your medical bills? How quickly can this drain your retirement?

Long-Term Care Rider

How do you intend to pay for long-term care? Will you sell off your assets, pay taxes, and then pay for services? I've seen family farms and businesses evaporate because of long-term care costs. There's a better way.

Long-term care insurance is expensive and is typically "use it or lose it." But life insurance is different. Many policies will give you an advance on your death benefit to pay for these expenses. This means you don't have to sell other assets, and you do not have to pay taxes. Different policies work differently. Some policies may reimburse you for expenses. Some policies may give you the money first and then require you to submit paperwork. Be sure to understand how your policy works.

Most people think of moving into a facility when they hear the term Long-Term Care. But Long-Term Care is much more than just moving into a facility.

Triggering events for long-term care insurance generally include difficulties in:
- Bathing
- Mobility
- Getting Dresses
- Using the toilet
- Eating

Other services provided by a caregiver could include:

- Shopping for groceries and clothes
- Taking medication
- Housework
- Care for pets

Unfortunately, few advisors talk to their clients about Long-Term Care until it's too late. Most folks don't quite understand what Long-Term Care is and what all is involved with it. What are the odds that you'll need Long-Term Care? Well, let's see.

- The odds of having a fire at your home is 1 in 1200. Yet, you're required by law to have fire insurance.
- The odds of getting into a car accident are about 1 in 240. And you know we all are required to have car insurance.
- But the startling thing is that the odds of you needing Long-Term Care is 1 in 2 . . . 1 in 2! Yet, we are not required to have Long-Term Care insurance.

There is a misalignment of needs. You're forced by law to purchase insurance for these things, yet Long-Term Care is a much more significant risk that you'll need, but not be required to have.

Ten million people each year need some form of Long-Term Care
- 37 percent are under the age of sixty-five
- 63 percent are over the age of sixty-five
- There is a 70 percent chance of having a long-term care event during your lifetime.
- On average, women need care for 3.7 years, and men need care for 2.2 years. One-third of today's sixty-five-year-olds may never need long-term care, but 20 percent will need it longer than five years.

The Costs of Long-Term Care

The average annual cost today of nursing-home is $94,896 per year. In ten years, it is expected to be $127,536 per year.

Some average Long-Term Care costs:

- $225 a day; $6,844 per month. It depends on the state and quality of the facility. Private or semi-private rooms can cost $7,698 per room
- $68 per day for services in an adult day health care center
- $20 an hour for homemaker services
- $3,628 per month for care in an assisted living facility

Who will provide the care, and how will you pay for it? Which family member is going to give up their life to provide care? The common way to pay for this is to sell assets and pay taxes on those assets. What if you could keep those assets and have other sources of cash flow to pay those expenses, and you don't have to pay taxes?

Longevity, with the inclusion of inflation and Long-Term Care, is a huge risk to consider during retirement. You need to make sure you have enough money throughout retirement to address these issues.

What's the Solution?

There's as two ways you can solve this problem.
- A Long-Term Care policy, but these policies are normally use-it-or-lose-it, and often you can't qualify for a policy due to health reasons.
- With a properly structured life insurance policy, you can take an early advance on the death benefit to pay for expenses.

Chapter 10
Life Insurance Retirement Plan

Creating a Tax-Free Retirement using an IUL

If you Google "Index Universal Life Insurance," or "IUL," you will find strong opinions about them. Many are in favor of them, and many are against them. Unfortunately, on either side of the debate, most truly don't understand the full truth. I am a big fan of IULS; when they are designed CORRECTLY, they are a phenomenal financial vehicle for retirement. If they are not designed correctly, then they are a horrific financial vehicle.

IULS are complicated financial vehicles. They offer a floor of 0, meaning you will never lose money, even when the stock market tanks. If the floor is zero, your cash value can still go down because of the cost of insurance and management fees associated with your policy. This cost isn't necessarily a problem because it offers you benefits, and your assets are protected. from wild losses in the stock market.

Many IUL policies, though not all, come with a guaranteed minimum interest rate of 1 or 2 percent. Some allow you to allocate your assets at a fixed rate of return. This ensures that your cash value will not decrease, regardless of how the selected index performs. This rate is specified in the policy, and it provides a baseline return.

I always allocate a portion of the money inside my IUL to the fixed account. I do this because there is a cost of insurance involved with life insurance. If the index produces no return for the policy, then the policy's cash value will be reduced because of the cost of insurance. By allocating a portion of the return to a fixed account, I will receive enough return inside the policy to pay for the cost of insurance.

The unique feature of IULs is the ability to earn additional interest based on the performance of a chosen stock market index. The insurance company calculates the interest credited by tracking the index's performance over a specific period, usually annually. Your policy may get 8% to 15% returns consistently, tax-free, when managed correctly. These returns are REAL returns, not *Average* returns. These consistent returns, with no market losses, make a significant difference to your wealth when compared to the up-and-down paper returns of a traditional retirement account.

Some Basics about IULs

Here is a hint: if you don't understand these basic terms and if you don't understand the difference between REAL returns and AVERAGE returns, it's a good idea to educate yourself before investing in an IUL or the stock market.

Floor or Spread:

Some policies also have a floor or spread, which means that even if the index has negative returns, your policy won't lose money. Instead, your return might be based on a minimum guaranteed interest rate or a spread over the index's performance.

Cap Rate and Participation Rate:

Insurance companies often set a cap rate, which is the maximum percentage of index gains that will be credited to your policy. For example, if the cap rate is 10 percent and the index gains 15 percent, your policy would be credited with a 10 percent return. Additionally, there might be a participation rate that determines the percentage of index gains you receive. If the participation rate is 80 percent and the index gains 10 percent, your policy would be credited with an 8 percent return.

They aren't doing this to screw you. It's a way to balance out the risks the insurance takes because, unlike a stock portfolio, your account doesn't go down. It's how they can guarantee you will never lose. When you read the chapter about average returns, you'll see the value in this.

Fees

There are a lot of lies out there about IUL fees, so I'll give you a summary. IULs are front-loaded with fees, just as many mutual funds are front-loaded. The cost of insurance does get more expensive as you get older, but there are ways to reduce those costs when you understand how IULs work and when you structure your IUL properly.

During your lifetime, you will pay more fees to your 401(k) provider or your financial advisor than you will pay for your IUL **IF** your IUL is designed for high cash value. Fees aren't necessarily a problem, IF they provide value and benefits. What benefits does a 401(k) and your financial advisor provide you?

- More risk of market losses.
- No access to capital
- No financial protection for Long-Term Care or pre-mature death
- Higher taxes.

If your policy is designed correctly, then the fees don't matter because the value, the growth, and the benefits will outweigh the fees. If it's designed incorrectly, then the fees will destroy the policy, so it's imperative that you understand how IULs operate, and it's imperative that you work with an advisor who knows how they work.

The cost of the insurance (COI) is based on many factors, including:
- Age
- Gender
- The risk of the insured.
- Net amount at risk.

The net amount at risk is defined as:
- the difference between the cash value and the death benefit amount.

For example. If your policy has $500,000 in death benefit and $350,000 in cash value, than the net amount at risk is $150,000. Although the death benefit is 500,000, the cost of insurance is based on 150,000 which is the risk to the insurance company.

When you design a policy with a high cash value, more of the money is going toward the cash accumulation and less is going toward the cost of insurance. But if you're wanting maximum cash value, there's only one way to do it correctly, and that is to buy the least amount of life insurance that the IRS allows and fund the policy right up to the Internal Revenue Code guidelines. Let's start with some basics. There are two types of policy costs within the contract. Fixed cost. And variable costs.

Fixed expenses are set amounts regardless of the death benefit. Amount that is purchased. There are two types of fixed expenses. Or a premium load, which is a sales charge and administration cost.

The premium load is a policy cost that is deducted off the top. Of the premium you pay, these costs are typically around 5 percent. These costs go toward any applicable state premium, tax, agent commissions, and profitability. Some companies will have a variable premium load schedule where the load percentage starts off higher but drops over time.

Others will have a level premium load percentage throughout the life of the policy. For example, if you pay a $100 premium into an IUL with a 5 percent premium load, $5 would come right off the top of your premium. The remaining $95 would be applied to your policy.

The administration cost is a monthly amount that exists for the life of the policy. This amount may range between $5 and $20 a month. This amount is considered a monthly deduction that is reduced from your policy cash value each month. The administration expense goes toward servicing the UL policy. In the form of enforced illustrations, policy anniversary statements, and enforced customer service.

Variable expenses are based on either the death benefit amount or the cash value accumulation. These costs vary based on how much death benefit is initially purchased, how much death benefit is carried throughout the life of the policy, and the performance of the cash value. Typical variable expenses include the cost of insurance and two expense charges. Number three: account value charge.

Can you use an IUL for a Family Banking System?

Yes, but I do not advocate for using an IUL as a *Family Banking System* or to borrow money against an IUL within at least the first 5-7 years. You can't use your money immediately like you can a whole life policy because you don't have access to as much capital immediately. Access to tax-free capital and keeping it growing uninterrupted are the foundations of this powerful financial strategy.

You don't have guarantees inside an IUL unless you allocate a portion to fixed returns. But you have the potential to earn more, and once the policy *seasons*, the arbitrage between your borrowed money, and your returns from the policy has the potential to be much greater than from a whole-life policy. You also must be more diligent about paying back the loans in the first couple of years.

What I like to do is start my clients off with a whole-life policy and build a solid foundation. I help them get out of debt using their policy. I help them get accustomed to borrowing and paying back the policy. I help them get to the point where they run all their money through their policy instead of keeping it parked in a bank.

I educate them on IULs. By the time they are ready for their second policy, some of them choose an IUL, but their focus is to use it as retirement plan, not a Family *Banking System*. By then, their debt is lower or gone, and they have a routine. They've become better stewards of their money. They aren't necessarily borrowing against their policy as much, unless they are a real estate investor or business owner.

Last Words on IULs

I cannot stress this enough. When working with life insurance, you must choose the correct agent, the correct product, and the correct company.

Different products are designed for different purposes. Some are for max income at retirement. Some are designed for max death benefit. Some are designed for estate planning. Some are designed for more Long-Term Care benefits.

If the person you're working with only offers you one company, then run. They don't have the ability to work for your best interest. If the person you're working with offers a company that sells home and auto insurance, then run. Those companies do not specialize in life insurance.

You want to work with a top-rated company that specializes in IULs and Whole Life Products. A good advisor should talk to you about two to three companies and contrast the differences.

If you are looking at term insurance, I still recommend the same advice. Many term policies allow you to convert them into whole life policies. Many policies do not. This because extraordinarily valuable as you get older and the risks of becoming uninsurable increase.

Chapter 11
What Else Can You use Life Insurance for?

Life insurance is a powerful asset. It's even used by businesses to pay executives and it's used in professional sports as part of contracts.

Banks and Corporations use properly structured permanent life insurance policies to attract, retain, and reward employees. It's also used to provide guaranteed tax-free income in retirement for employees and executives. Along the way, these accounts act as liquid assets, which can be utilized for cash reserves or a strategic investment when an opportunity presents itself.

You can do the same thing!

Corporate-owned life insurance-otherwise known as COLI- refers to life insurance purchased by a corporation for its use. The corporation is either the total, or the partial beneficiary of the policy, and an employee is the insured.

A few of the different ways COLI can be utilized:
- Key-Man Insurance
- Executive bonus plans.
- Retention Bonus Plans.
- Split-dollar arrangements.
- Salary deferral plans.
- Supplemental executive retirement plans.

Key Person Insurance

Do you have a key employee who is instrumental in your company's success? As a business owner, it's critical for you to do everything you can to provide these top performers with the type of executive benefits that will keep them loyal to your company today and for years to come.

The loss of a key employee can be detrimental to a business. This may be the loss of an owner, a sales rep, a top executive, or even someone who provides your business with some intellectual capacity.

The death of a shareholder or key person can financially strain a company in various ways. It is often challenging to replace a key person. Once found, it may be months or even years before that replacement can operate at the same level. This can be very disruptive to a business and cause problems with efficiency and profitability.

Life insurance can provide a business with the cash flow needed to shore up working capital, repay debts, or provide the funds necessary to hire and train a replacement when a key executive dies.

If a business partner dies, the deceased's family would be entitled to a share of the business. Life insurance, purchased as a funding mechanism for a buy-sell agreement, provides the business with the liquidity to buy out the deceased partner's interest from the family.

Section 162 Plan

A Section 162 plan, often referred to as an executive bonus plan, is a compensation arrangement used by businesses to provide additional benefits to key employees. This plan derives its name from Section 162 of the Internal Revenue Code, which allows businesses to deduct the bonuses paid under the plan as a business expense.

In a 162 plan, the employer selects key employees to participate in the program. These employees are typically executives or other individuals crucial to the company's success. The employer then offers these employees a bonus, which is used to purchase a life insurance policy. The policy is owned by the employee and provides a death benefit to their beneficiaries. This policy can be used to accumulate high cash value and be used as tax-free income in retirement.

One of the key features of a 162 plan is its flexibility. Unlike other employee benefit plans, such as a 401(k) or pension plan, a 162 plan does not have to meet specific regulatory requirements. This makes it easier for businesses to design a plan that meets the needs of their key employees. From the employee's perspective, a 162 plan offers several advantages.

Of course, this bonus is taxable. A business owner can pay the employee a "double bonus," which will provide enough money to the employee to pay both the insurance premiums and taxes on the bonus.

Benefits for employers:
- Help attract and retain top talent at a relatively low cost.
- Bonuses given to employees to pay the whole life premium are tax deductible (the policy premium is taxable for the employee).

Benefits for employees:
- The cash value of the whole life policy can be accessed at any time.
- Upon retirement, employees may use the cash value to supplement retirement.

Fully Insured Plan 412 (E)(3)

This is a less well-known strategy because you need a lot of money to capitalize on it. Its contributions can be upward of $275,000 or more. These plans also allow you to avoid Medicare and Social Security taxes.

Unlike other retirement plans, the IRS does not determine the contribution limits for the 412 (E) (3) plan. Instead, they are determined by the actuary, who designs a plan and calculates the contribution limits based on the plan design and benefits provided. Therefore, the contribution limits can vary widely depending on individual circumstances and the plans assigned. The limits are based on a specific formula.

A good candidate for this plan is a small business owner who desires a large current tax deduction and secure guaranteed retirement income. Unfortunately, most tax-professional financial planners are unfamiliar with the strategy.

Most retirement plans are 100 percent dictated by the stock market. But rather than using the plan assets to invest in stocks, bonds, and mutual funds, the plan benefits are guaranteed with insurance contracts, including life insurance.

- Tax savings: delivers significant tax deductions year over year.
- Guaranteed income: offers pre-determined retirement income.
- No investment risk: the insurance company providing the funding vehicle bears all investment risk.
- Insulated from volatility: The value of your plan assets is insulated from market fluctuation
- Additional protection: You can buy life insurance through the plan.
- Protection from creditors: Assets from your fully insured plan are typically protected from creditors.

RETENTION BONUS

A retention bonus using life insurance involves an employer providing a life insurance policy as an incentive for an employee to remain with the company for a predetermined period. The policy is typically paid for by the employer and is separate from the employee's regular compensation package. The key feature of this type of bonus is that it provides a long-term benefit to the employee, as the policy can continue even after the employee leaves the company, provided they meet certain conditions.

How Does It Work?

When an employee is offered a retention bonus using life insurance, they are usually required to stay with the company for a specified number of years to fully vest in the policy. If the employee leaves before the vesting period ends, they may forfeit some or all the benefits. Once the vesting period is complete, the employee becomes the owner of the policy and can continue it by paying the premiums themselves, even if they leave the company.

Benefits for Employees

- Financial Security: Life insurance provides financial security for the employee's loved ones in the event of their death, which can be a valuable benefit.
- Long-Term Investment: The policy can serve as a long-term investment, providing a source of income or a financial cushion in retirement.
- Portability: Typically, the policy can be taken with the employee if they leave the company, providing continued coverage without the need to reapply for insurance.

Benefits for Employers

- Employee Retention: Offering a retention bonus in the form of life insurance can help companies retain valuable employees, reducing turnover costs.
- Cost-Effective: Life insurance premiums may be tax-deductible for the employer, making this type of bonus cost-effective compared to cash bonuses.
- Attractive Benefit: Life insurance can be an attractive benefit for employees, helping companies attract top talent.

SALARY DEFRRAL PLANS

A salary deferral plan using life insurance, often referred to as a deferred compensation plan, is a type of executive benefit plan that allows employees to defer a portion of their salary into a life insurance policy. These plans are typically used by high-income earners, such as executives or business owners, to supplement their retirement savings and provide additional death benefits to their beneficiaries.

How Salary Deferral Plans Work

In a salary deferral plan using life insurance, participating employees choose to defer a portion of their salary, bonuses, or other compensation into a life insurance policy. The deferred amount is not included in the employee's taxable income for the year in which it is earned, providing immediate tax savings. The funds within the policy grow tax-deferred until they are withdrawn. Upon your employee's retirement, your business makes retirement income payments according to the terms of the agreement. These payments are taxable income to your retired employee and tax-deductible by your business. There are some IRS reporting requirements.

If your key employee dies before reaching retirement, your business receives the policy's death benefit income tax-free and pays survivor benefits to the employee's designated beneficiaries. These payments are deductible by your business and reportable as taxable income to the beneficiaries.

Your business may choose how to cover the cost of paying your participating employee's retirement benefits. Policy cash values can be used through loans and/or withdrawals to make the required payments. Alternatively, your business can pay the benefits from current cash flow and cost recover the benefit payments through eventual receipt of the death proceeds from the life insurance policy.

Types of Life Insurance Policies Used

Employers can offer different types of life insurance policies for these plans, including whole life, universal life, or variable life insurance. Each type of policy has its own features and benefits, so employees should carefully consider their options before making a decision.

Benefits of Salary Deferral Plans Using Life Insurance

- Tax Advantages: Contributions to the plan are tax-deferred, meaning employees do not pay income tax on the deferred amount until it is withdrawn. This can result in significant tax savings over time.
- Death Benefits: The life insurance policy provides a death benefit to the employee's beneficiaries. This can provide financial security to loved ones in the event of the employee's death.
- Cash Value Growth: The cash value within the life insurance policy grows tax-deferred, similar to a retirement account. This can help employees build a substantial nest egg over time.

- Creditor Protection: In many cases, the cash value within a life insurance policy is protected from creditors, providing an additional layer of financial security.
- Flexible Withdrawal Options: Employees can typically access the cash value within the policy through loans or withdrawals, providing flexibility in how they use the funds.

SERP

A SERP, or Supplemental Executive Retirement Plan, is a type of arrangement that companies use to provide additional retirement benefits for key employees. It typically involves using life insurance as a funding vehicle, among other financial tools.

Understanding SERPs:

A SERP is a non-qualified retirement plan, meaning it does not have to meet the same regulatory requirements as qualified plans like 401(k)s. This gives companies more flexibility in designing and funding the plan, making it particularly attractive for rewarding and retaining top talent. SERPs are usually offered to key executives or employees who are not part of a company's standard retirement plan or whose contributions are limited due to IRS rules.

Role of Life Insurance:

Life insurance is often used in SERPs to fund future benefit payments. The company purchases a life insurance policy on the key executive's life, with the company as the owner and beneficiary of the policy. The cash value of the policy grows over time, and when the executive retires or passes away, the company can use the policy's proceeds to fund the promised retirement benefits.

If your key employee dies before reaching retirement, your business receives the policy's death benefit income tax-free and pays survivor benefits to the employee's designated beneficiaries. These payments are deductible by your business and reportable as taxable income to the beneficiaries.

Advantages for Employees:

For employees, SERPs can be highly attractive. They provide an additional retirement income stream that is not subject to the same contribution limits as qualified plans. SERPs can also offer greater flexibility in retirement planning, as the benefits are typically paid out as a lump sum or over a shorter period than traditional pensions. Additionally, the life insurance component can provide a death benefit to the executive's beneficiaries, providing financial security in the event of their untimely death.

Advantages for Employers:

Employers benefit from SERPs by being able to attract and retain top talent. By offering additional retirement benefits, companies can incentivize key employees to stay with the organization for the long term. SERPs can also be structured to provide tax advantages for the company, as contributions to the plan are tax-deductible and the growth of the life insurance policy's cash value is tax-deferred.

Phantom Stock

It's a type of Supplemental Executive Retirement Plan (SERP) where the key employee's retirement benefit is tied to the corporation's stock. This type of plan can help top performers commit to their company for the long term. And the plan can be funded with life insurance.

Phantom stock is a type of deferred compensation plan where employees receive hypothetical units that mimic the value of company shares. These units typically track the performance of the company's stock price over time. When the employee reaches a certain milestone, such as retirement or a specified number of years of service, they receive a payout based on the value of the phantom stock units.

How companies benefit

- The business owner can select which employees will participate.
- The business owner can tie the benefit to corporate growth—without sacrificing their equity in the company.
- Benefits can be customized for each participating executive.
- The life insurance policy grows tax-deferred and is listed as an asset in the corporation's books.
- The plan is relatively easy to implement.

How employees benefit

- The employee will receive a benefit that's tied to the performance of the company over the long term.
- The benefit is not taxable until it is received.

How Does It Work with Life Insurance?

In a phantom stock plan using life insurance, the company purchases a life insurance policy for the employee's life, with the company as the beneficiary. The value of the policy is often tied to the value of the phantom stock units. If the employee passes away while covered by the policy, the company receives the death benefit, which can then be used to fund the payouts to the employee's beneficiaries.

How does this strategy work?

Phantom Stock Plans come in two general forms: a "stock appreciation" plan and a "mirror" plan:

- With a stock appreciation plan, key employees who are selected to participate are credited with a specific number of hypothetical shares by the business. These hypothetical shares have a value set at the time the participant becomes a participant in the plan. Instead of transferring actual shares to the employee, the business creates an accounting entry in which plan participants are credited with a specified number of "shares" whose value may rise or fall over time according to the formula selected to determine value. At the end of a specified time period or upon predetermined events, such as death or disability, the employee is entitled to receive the value based only on the appreciation of the hypothetical shares they were credited with.

- With a mirror plan, the benefit is based on the total value of the hypothetical stock—including all appreciation from inception. So at the end of the specified time period, the value of the benefit is based on the total value of the hypothetical stock, not just the growth.

Benefits for Employees

- Retirement Planning: Phantom stock plans can serve as a valuable retirement planning tool, providing employees with a source of income upon retirement.
- Deferred Taxation: Employees are not taxed on the value of the phantom stock units until they receive a payout, allowing for tax-deferred growth.
- Incentive Alignment: Since the value of the phantom stock is tied to the company's performance, employees are motivated to work toward the company's success.
- Risk Mitigation: The life insurance component provides a financial safety net for the employee's beneficiaries in the event of their death.

Benefits for Employers

- Retention and Motivation: Phantom stock plans can help retain key employees by providing them with a valuable incentive to stay with the company.
- Cost-Effective: Compared to traditional stock options, phantom stock plans can be more cost-effective for companies as they do not involve the actual transfer of ownership.
- Flexibility: Companies have the flexibility to design phantom stock plans that suit their specific needs and objectives.
- Tax Deductions: Companies may be able to deduct the cost of the phantom stock plan, including the premiums paid for the life insurance policy, as a business expense.

Chapter 12
Business Succession Planning

You will leave your business at some point.

The question is, will YOU leave your business on your time and on your terms, or will you leave your business on someone else's time and on their terms?

I want you to live your life to the max. Get that bucket list out and get on it! But I also must give you the bad news: You will eventually die, and I don't know when. So, get your act together, and don't leave a mess for your family to deal with!

You may not die before you leave your business, but you will leave your business at some point. Is your family prepared to take it over if needed? Are they prepared to sell it if needed? How will they get top dollar? How will they sell it with the least amount of tax burden?

Succession planning is the process of preparing and transferring the ownership and management of a business or asset to the next generation or successor. Establishing a succession plan aims to ensure the smooth transition of control and ownership of your business and wealth to the next generation. Doing all this while maintaining family harmony, minimizing taxes, and ensuring the business survives the transition can be accomplished with proper planning. Unfortunately, many business owners and individuals neglect succession planning, leading to significant tax problems.

When one shareholder dies, their company shares must be transferred to someone else (typically a family member). This transfer can trigger a host of tax consequences for both the shareholder and the business itself. As such, it's important to consult with a tax advisor before making decisions about succession planning.

A "surprise succession plan" can cause much confusion and fighting among the people who might take over. It can cause your family to pay more taxes than they legally must. It may even shut down the business, bankrupt your family, or both. The entity structure of a business can have a significant impact on succession planning, estate planning, and your family's tax burden.

If you're a partnership, succession planning is more complex. This is because multiple owners and families are involved, each with their own vested interests in the business. When one owner dies, the surviving owner(s) must decide what to do with the deceased owner's share of the business. The good news is that with proper planning, a properly funded buy-sell agreement can resolve many issues. A properly funded buy-sell agreement may allow the family of the departing business to walk away with money from the business.

What is a Buy-Sell Agreement, and Why Do I Need One?

A buy-sell agreement is a legally binding contract that provides for the transfer of ownership in the business upon a "triggering event" such as death, disability, retirement, divorce, bankruptcy, or any other reason an owner may leave their business.

Working with tax and legal counsel, the owners of a business (and possibly the business itself) enter into a written agreement that provides rights and obligations for purchasing a business owner's interest in the business should one of the specified triggering events occur. The owner, in turn, agrees that they (or their estate, in the case of death) will transfer the business interest to the other owners (or the business itself) for an agreed-upon price.

By implementing a buy-sell agreement, the business is more likely to continue running smoothly after the departure. It ensures the business will remain in the other owner's control and may reduce the need to work with any outside parties. A buy-sell agreement also protects the departing owner and their family. There is a designated buyer for their interest in the business if a triggering event occurs, which means the owner (or their estate) can be fairly compensated for their interest in the business.

The Basic Questions a Buy/Sell Agreement Should Answer

- Is the agreement between all the owners or just some owners?
- What are the triggering events for the buy-sell obligations?
- Who can buy the owner's interest in the business?
- How will the price of the departing owner's interest be determined?

Is your buy-sell adequately funded?

Typically, a buy-sell agreement should have provisions that address how the remaining owners will pay the departing owner. Common methods for funding a purchase obligation include:
- An installment sale
- Creating a sinking fund of investments for a future purchase
- Borrowing money
- Life insurance is the preferred method of funding.

Who will take over the business?

- Do you want to leave your business to a family member?
- Are there co-owners?
- Does a key employee want to take over the business?
- Would this person be able to purchase the business from you? Would you want them to buy it, or would you rather have the business go to them?
- In the case of a divorce, a new partner? The Bank? A new partner?
- What about if you are disabled?
- Do you own a business that requires a license, such as a C.P.A. firm, Real Estate Brokerage, or Insurance Agency?
- Does one owner provide a skill or the financial backing another owner cannot?
- How will the new owner get the funding needed?
- Why are they no longer able to serve in that role?

Chapter 13
How Your Family Banking System and Real Estate are similar

1. Both are great warehouses for your wealth

2. Both provide positive cashflow

3. Appreciation: a consistent and predictable increase in wealth

4. Tax benefits

5. Deposits create equity

6. Access to capital

7. Both provide retirement income

8. Both increase family wealth

9. Both hedge against inflation because they are growing at a rate similar to, or higher than, inflation

10. Your tenants pay for it

    Your tenants pay for your real estate. If you run your capital through your Family Banking System, you can use that to fund cash-flowing real estate. Real estate is going to kick off cash flow that you can use to repay the policy and fund another policy, and so it's a cycle that perpetuates itself. On one side, the cash value of life insurance supports real estate, and on the other side, the cash flow from that supports the life insurance policy. Together, your wealth is growing in two places at the same time.

11. You can rent it

    One of the great benefits of owning real estate is the ability to rent out your property and have someone else pay off the property through rent payments.

    With a life insurance policy, you don't have a building to rent out, but you can rent your money in the form of a loan.

12. It's an Asset You Can Sell

You can sell real estate at any point in time. There are fees associated with that. Whether you use a realtor or a buyer's agent, you end up incurring some type of cost.

Life insurance works similarly. Your policy is an asset that you own, similar to your deed. The courts have ruled that you can sell it as well. Those are called life settlements. You can sell them just like real estate. Another big point of similarity is the sale and transfer of contracts. Yes! Mortgage notes can be sold and traded. The same thing is with life insurance policies—it is called viatical settlements or life settlements.

13. Collateralization

Banks love to lend money on both real estate and life insurance. If you have a certain net worth and income level, banks will lend you money to pay premiums for a life insurance policy. This is called premium financing.Premium financing uses borrowed money to pay for life insurance premiums. enabling the policy owner to avoid tying up their own capital to pay premiums. Instead, they use that capital as collateral for the loan.

Chapter 14
Why the Average Returns of Your Portfolio Do Not Matter

"Rule number 1: Never lose money. Rule number 2: Never forget rule number 1"
—WARREN BUFFET

I learned a long time ago in helping a corporate client select an investment manager that average returns are pretty meaningless and that a higher average return doesn't mean you will have more money. The key is the extent of the ups and downs and when you are doing your scoring up and measuring, and that exercise taught me that it's a lot more important to have less dramatic ups and downs, unless you like riding roller coasters. -
—TED BENNA (Father of the 401(k))

Have you ever noticed that no matter what the market is doing, whether it's skyrocketing, plummeting, or staying level, your money is always supposed to remain in the market? It is as if this is the only way your money can grow, and the only way you can have money in retirement. Why is that?

You've heard it all:
- You're in it for the long haul.
- Don't take it out: it's increasing.
- You can't sell it; it's only a paper loss. You'll gain it back.
- The market will come back.
- It's not a loss until you sell it.

These are all scare tactics to keep your money locked up in the stock market and giving access of your money to someone else. If I were to choose one of the most detrimental financial myths, it would be this: The *average* return of your portfolio is important. It is not. It's essential to recognize that the average rate of return has absolutely no significance on how much money you keep when you invest.

Traditional financial planning requires you to focus on your portfolio's average rate of return. While the financial industry is having you focus on *average* returns and your 401 (k), Wall Street is busy making trillions of dollars off you and is controlling your money throughout your lifetime.

Suppose you have $1,000,000 and you have a choice to keep your money in an account that will give you an average rate of return of 25% or keep an account that'll give you a 5% return every year. Which would you choose? Without hesitation, most folks will choose the account that gives them an *average* return of 25%. But is that a wise decision? Let's look.

In the first year, you get a 100% rate of return, and you double your money. In the second year, you lose 50%, and you're back down to the same $1 million you started with. However, in year 3, you have another great year, and you're back to $2,000,000. Unfortunately, in year 4, you lose another 50%

	Average ROR: 25.00%	%	Actual Net IRR: .00%		
	Cash Flow 1:				
	Cash Flow 2:				
	Cash Flow 3:				
Year	Beg. Of Year Account Value	Earnings Rate	Interest Earnings	End of Year Account Value	
1	1,000,000	100.00%	1,000,000	2,000,000	
2	2,000,000	(50.00%)	(1,000,000)	1,000,000	
3	1,000,000	100.00%	1,000,000	2,000,000	
4	2,000,000	(50.00%)	(1,000,000)	1,000,000	

So, what happens in that time frame? There is no gain on your money. If you're paying a 1% fee, in years 1 and 3, you'll pay about $20,000 yearly per year in fees, and in years 2 and 4, you'll pay about $10,000 per year in fees

So, you'll pay about $60,000 in fees and lose money. Depending on the type of account, you may have some taxes. And, of course, you have opportunity cost because your money has been sitting there for four years doing nothing for you except losing value due to inflation.

I'm telling you this because a financial advisor will tell you what a great job you've done, and you'll like the 25% Average Return. Even though the average rate of return was 25%, the actual rate of return was 0, or negative after fees and taxes.

This is some of that fuzzy math that allows Wall Street to legitimately, legally, and mathematically show how you have a 25% Average return and yet lose money. But frankly, it doesn't work.

What about the 5% account? In our example, the account that earned a 5 % rate of return outperformed the account that earned a 25% rate of return. Why is that? It's because there are no losses. The Average rate of return will always be higher than the real Rate of Return because it does not show the impact losses have.

A BLUEPRINT FOR BUILDING WEALTH THROUGH THE TAX CODE

| | Average ROR: 5.00% | % | Actual Net IRR: 5.00% |

| Cash Flow 1: |
| Cash Flow 2: |
| Cash Flow 3: |

Year	Beg. Of Year Account Value	Earnings Rate	Interest Earnings	End of Year Account Value
1	1,000,000	5.00%	50,000	1,050,000
2	1,050,000	5.00%	52,500	1,102,500
3	1,102,500	5.00%	55,125	1,157,625
4	1,157,625	5.00%	57,881	1,215,506

Let's look at one more example.

In our left example, we look at the market returns from 1961 to 1987. We start with $160,000 and end up with $680,337. The average return is 6.67%.

Year	Account Value	Earnings Rate	Account Value
1	160,000	23.13%	197,006
2	197,006	(11.81%)	173,739
3	173,739	18.89%	206,560
4	206,560	12.97%	233,351
5	233,351	9.06%	254,497
6	254,497	(13.09%)	221,181
7	221,181	20.09%	265,620
8	265,620	7.66%	285,968
9	285,968	(11.36%)	253,478
10	253,478	0.10%	253,726
11	253,726	10.79%	281,094
12	281,094	15.63%	325,039
13	325,039	(17.37%)	268,594
14	268,594	(29.72%)	188,773
15	188,773	31.55%	248,329
16	248,329	19.15%	295,880
17	295,880	(11.50%)	261,848
18	261,848	1.06%	264,629
19	264,629	12.31%	297,202
20	297,202	25.77%	373,801
21	373,801	(9.73%)	337,429
22	337,429	14.76%	387,238
23	387,238	17.27%	454,118
24	454,118	1.40%	460,478
25	460,478	26.33%	581,738
26	581,738	14.62%	666,763
27	666,763	2.04%	680,337

Year	Account Value	Earnings Rate	Account Value
1	160,000	6.67%	170,672
2	170,672	6.67%	182,056
3	182,056	6.67%	194,199
4	194,199	6.67%	207,152
5	207,152	6.67%	220,969
6	220,969	6.67%	235,708
7	235,708	6.67%	251,429
8	251,429	6.67%	268,200
9	268,200	6.67%	286,089
10	286,089	6.67%	305,171
11	305,171	6.67%	325,526
12	325,526	6.67%	347,238
13	347,238	6.67%	370,399
14	370,399	6.67%	395,105
15	395,105	6.67%	421,458
16	421,458	6.67%	449,569
17	449,569	6.67%	479,556
18	479,556	6.67%	511,542
19	511,542	6.67%	545,662
20	545,662	6.67%	582,057
21	582,057	6.67%	620,881
22	620,881	6.67%	662,293
23	662,293	6.67%	706,468
24	706,468	6.67%	753,590
25	753,590	6.67%	803,854
26	803,854	6.67%	857,471
27	857,471	6.67%	914,665

On the right, we start with $160,000 and end up with $914,000, and the average rate of return is the same. Why the difference? Again, Losses. A 20% loss has a much more significant impact on your bottom line than a 20% paper return.

Looking at the chart on the right, you will notice that it always increases in value. When you sit down with a financial advisor, they'll show you are chart that goes up, up, up. They proceed to tell you if you put *this much money* into the market and it gets *this return,* you'll have *this much money.* They may even tell you that the market gains will make up for market losses. Well, math doesn't work this way.

The market has indeed increased over history, but it doesn't matter what **THE MARKET** has done since its inception. It only matters what **YOUR** portfolio has done during your lifetime. What is most important is what **YOUR** portfolio does in the five to seven years **BEFORE** your retirement and the five to seven years **AFTER** your retirement.

If you look at a historical graph of the S&P 500, you'll discover that the stock market crash in the early 1900s dropped nearly 70% and took 26 years to recover. The stock market crash of 1929 fell 89% and took almost 29 years to recover. The stock market crash of 1969 dropped nearly 69% and took 29 years to recover. From December 1996 to March 2000, it went up almost 100% just to lose 50%. Let's take a look at some other numbers:

- March 2020 Corona Virus: The market lost 20%. Since 2020, the value of the dollar has dropped nearly 20%.
- 2008-2009 Housing Bubble: 50% in 17 months (The market took around four years to Recover; Total Dollar Depreciation 3%)
- 2000-2003.Com Bust: The market declined by38%, and took nearly 4 Years to Recover. The dollar depreciated almost 10%.
- 1998: Currency Crises: The market declined by 13%
- 1990-1991 Recession: The market declined 17% in 3 months
- 1987 Stock Market Crash: Oct 19, 1987, The market declined 23%, which led ed to the Savings and
- Loan Crisis of 1989; Total Dollar Depreciation 14%.
- 1980-1982: The market declined 16% and the value of dollar depreciated by 22.5%.
- 1973-1975: The market declined 45%, and the value of Dollar Depreciated 22%.
- 1970: The market declined 30% Dec 3, 1968-May 26, 1970.
- 1962 Missile Crisis: The market declined 26.5%.
- Great Depression: The market declined 89 % in four years, and took nearly 29 years to Recover)
- Volatility during the early 1900s and finally crashed

Your advisor isn't wrong when they tell you the market will come back. But they aren't being honest with you. The market will always come back, but how long will it take, and how much wealth do you lose? If you look at history, it can take anywhere from a couple of years to a few decades.

What happens to your money while the market is losing value or recovering? Wall Street is using your money to create wealth. Your advisor is getting paid. You're losing value due to inflation; you're losing opportunity cost from all the money you're losing. It sounds like Wall Street is winning.

The average rate of return is used to evaluate the historical performance of an investment period; it measures history. It doesn't measure the future or how much money you'll have in retirement. It doesn't consider taxes, fees, inflation, the timing of your losses or the magnitude of your losses. It doesn't consider the changing markets, governments, or economies. All these factors have a more significant impact on investment returns than the average rate of return.

Want to do more research? Here are some more resources.

- The average Rate of Return means nothing. It's when you start investing and stop investing- NY Times.
- *Investors often have expectations of actual annual returns greater than 7 percent – the areas in green. But over 20 years or longer, rates that high are rare.*

—*New York Times*

http://archive.nytimes.com/www.nytimes.com/interactive/2011/01/02/business/20110102-metrics-graphic.html?ref=business

- What's the cost?
- Compounding the losses
- Inflation
- Opportunity Cost
- How long it takes to regain your original investment

TRUTH: You can't recover from lost time and opportunity.

- *The overall market is highly volatile and affected by generally long cycles. Ten, twenty, or even thirty years is not long enough to ensure successful returns in the market.* – Crestmont Research

https://www.crestmontresearch.com/

- *After 60 or 70 years, returns are relatively stable, but this time frame is longer than the relevant horizon for many retirement plans.* —New York Times
- "After accounting for dividends, inflation, taxes, and fees, $10,000 invested at the end of 1961 would have shrunk to $6,600 by 1981. From the end of 1979 to 1999, $10,000 would have grown to $48,000." New York Times. What Does this tell you? The Stock Market is about TIMING, not long-term investing.

http://archive.nytimes.com/www.nytimes.com/interactive/2011/01/02/business/20110102-metrics-graphic.html?ref=business

Are you ready to increase your wealth, protect your assets, and pay less in taxes?

Reach Out

Andrew Keehn

785.430.3717